Gertrude Jekyll

Her Art Restored
at Upton Grey

The Manor House
UPTON GREY
Hampshire

Gertrude Jekyll

*Her Art Restored
at Upton Grey*

Rosamund Wallinger

GARDEN • ART • PRESS

**To Professor Michael Tooley, Hampshire Gardens Trust
and all those who have helped me with this great adventure**

British Library Cataloguing–in–Publication Data
A catalogue record for this book is available from the British Library

Front cover: *Jonathan Myles-Lea's portrait of the garden and churchyard*
Endpapers Front: *The Rose Garden*
Back: *The Wild Garden*
Title page: *Rose archway to the Kitchen Garden*
Frontispiece: *The wall under Border 3 in June*

Printed in China for Garden Art Press, a division of the
Antique Collectors' Club Ltd.

CONTENTS

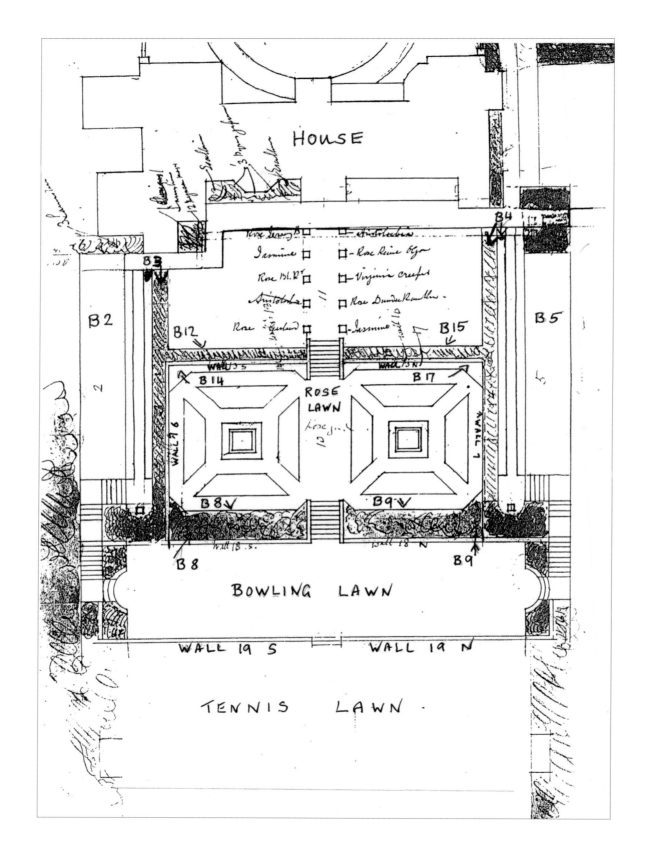

HOUSE

B4

B3

B2

B12

Rose Jeruy   Aristolochia

Jasmine   Rose Reine Olga

Rose Bl. R?   Virginia creeper

Aristolochia   Rose Dundee Rambler.

Rose Garland   Jasmine

B15

B5

WALL 3 S

WALL 3 N

B14

B17

ROSE
LAWN

WALL 6

WALL 7

B8

B9

WALL 18 S

WALL 18 N

B8

B9

BOWLING   LAWN

WALL 19 S   WALL 19 N

TENNIS   LAWN.

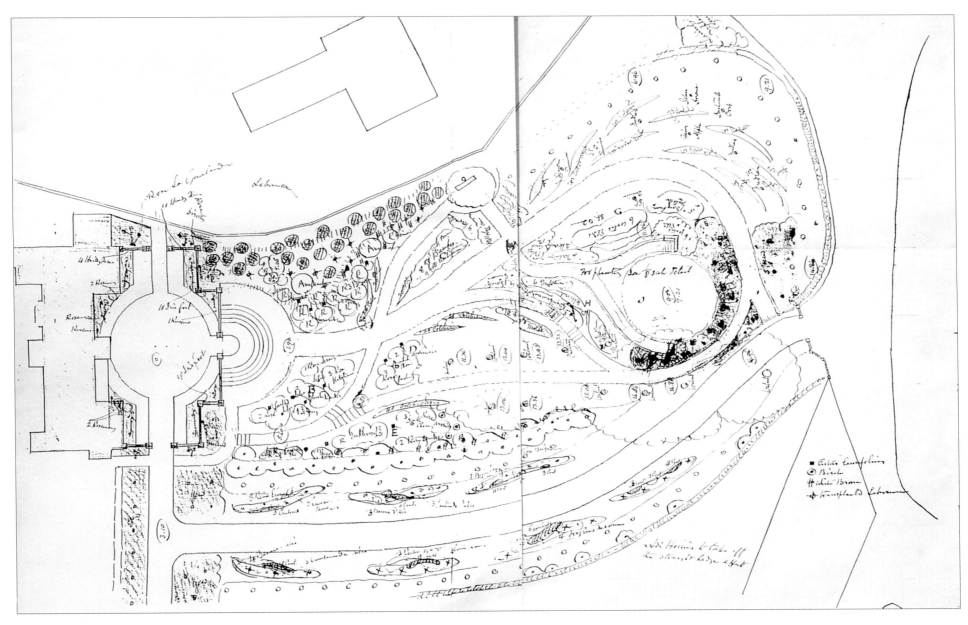

Gertrude Jekyll's plan for the Wild Garden

Opposite: Gertrude Jekyll's plan for the Formal Garden

INTRODUCTION

Obituary The Times 8.12.1932

'We regret to announce that Miss Gertrude Jekyll died at her home at Godalming on Thursday evening,
at the age of 89....She was a great gardener, second only, if indeed she was second, to her friend William Robinson
of Gravetye. To these two, more than to any others are due, not only the complete transformation of
English horticultural method and design, but also that wide diffusion of knowledge and taste
which has made us almost a nation of gardeners.
Miss Jekyll was also a true artist with an exquisite sense of colour.'

Gertrude Jekyll

This book is a visual record of a restored Gertrude Jekyll garden. Its purpose is to illustrate today and for future generations, exactly why Miss Jekyll was so admired in her lifetime, and why she continues to inspire and influence gardeners today.

A garden that is restored exactly to the one hundred-year-old original plans could be considered unnatural in its static, unchanging style, but Upton Grey is unique in that it represents a museum in garden art. It gives today's gardeners an opportunity to see, judge and learn from a garden of another era, and from this information to evolve their own art.

To date Upton Grey is one of the very few complete and fully restored Gertrude Jekyll gardens. Amongst others Lindisfarne Castle garden on Holy Island, off the coast of Northumberland (a smaller and therefore limited design) and Hestercombe garden in Somerset are important. Upton Grey is a valuable, rich and living example of her art.

Perhaps gardening is the most ephemeral of the arts, but it is sometimes the most easily restored. There can be few better environments than the British Isles for aspiring gardeners who wish to create or restore a garden. The advice available is invaluable and plentiful. We can turn to help from county gardens trusts, The Royal Horticultural Society and The Royal Botanic Gardens at Kew in London, amongst others. Our climate is relatively benign and we have an eclectic assortment of soils in which to grow the plants that

we have accumulated from around the world and the new cultivars that we breed. Changing climates, new plant material, viruses and social conditions will obviously influence the design of future gardens.

This Jekyll garden will probably change, deteriorate and revive with each generation of owners, but as long as it is not physically damaged (with buildings and hard structures) it can die back and grow again naturally. In my experience a period of disintegration and return to rampant nature may improve the garden's long-term chances of survival. As long as plans remain available and the plant material is not lost, it may do the earth good to undergo years of neglect.

So here, almost 30 years after the start of its restoration, is a complete picture of the garden Miss Jekyll designed in 1908 and 1909.

When we moved to Upton Grey in 1984 there were effectively no plants left growing in their original places. We had to restore beds completely, double dig and manure them and we then had to refer to plantsmen around England (sometimes around the world) to find the exact species and cultivars. Where possible we grew from seeds, but where necessary we bought plants, and these tended to prove stronger than the few survivors from the 1909 garden.

We are fortunate to have been given copies of photographs taken of the garden before and shortly after Miss Jekyll planned it in late 1908 and early 1909. As far as I can judge from those black and white pictures, this garden is now truer to Miss Jekyll's plans than it has ever been.

The Manor House now holds copies of all her plans for the Upton Grey garden as well as pages from her notebooks that list the many plants she supplied from her nursery at Munstead Wood. For those reasons and because Gertrude Jekyll's books, articles and the biographies of her give a full picture of the woman, the era in which she gardened and her achievements, I am concentrating on a description and understanding of her art.

In 1908 the owner of the Manor House was Charles Holme (1848-1923), founder of the influential Arts and Crafts magazine, *The Studio*. His great granddaughter, Toni Huberman, has written an enlightening account of his life for The Japan Society's *British and Japanese 'Biographical Portraits.'* I have enjoyed reading about the interesting figure who may have been responsible for making The Manor House and its five acre garden a small monument to the Arts and Crafts movement.

This is predominantly a pictorial record and I am grateful to Dick Longfield for photographing the garden so carefully through the seasons. The University of California at Berkeley have kindly allowed me to print copies of the garden plans which form part of their Reef Point Collection.

Mrs Martin McLaren has been a source of generous encouragement and support to me over the years. She is responsible for amassing and cataloguing a valuable collection of Jekylliana which confirms my admiration for Miss Jekyll's art in so many fields, particularly her mastery of design.

The Jekyll Trust have proved an invaluable help to me and have allowed me to use material for which they hold copyright.

A valuable contribution to this book is made by Professor Michael Tooley. He has written a chapter on Miss Jekyll's discovery, admiration and use of Mediterranean plants, a facet of her art that has been rather neglected.

I am particularly grateful to Penelope Hobhouse, Richard Bisgrove and Hampshire Gardens Trust for continued support in this adventure. Jonathan Myles-Lea has kindly permitted me to use his fine garden portrait.

So, because we have copies of all Miss Jekyll's plans and plant

lists and so many relevant photographs, this book provides a truly unique recording of her eclectic, imaginative and inspiring art.

Miss Jekyll described garden art as 'painting the landscape with living material'. I hope you will agree that her garden at Upton Grey makes a beautiful picture.

George Leslie wrote a touching description of his neighbour and friend in *Our River*

'Clever and witty in conversation, active and energetic in mind and body, and possessed of artistic talents of no common order...there is hardly any handicraft the mysteries of which she has not mastered – carving, modelling, house-painting, carpentry, smith's work, repoussé work, gilding, wood-inlaying, embroidery, gardening, and all manner of herb and flower knowledge and culture, everything being carried on with perfect method and completeness.'

The view to the house from tennis lawn in midsummer, showing the balance between the planted dry-stone walls and the architecture. One of the precepts of the Arts & Crafts movement was that art and craft should complement each other.

CHAPTER ONE

The Garden from 1902 to the Start of its Restoration in 1984

*'The Garden is a Grand Teacher. It teaches patience and careful watchfulness.
It teaches industry and thrift and above all it teaches entire trust.'* Wood and Garden

Aerial view of the house and garden. The contrast between Formal and Free or Wild styles is evident here. To the north of the house grass paths wind through trees, shrubs and wild flowers towards a pond. To the south, straight lines enclose each area, showing Miss Jekyll's eclectic art.

The garden of The Manor House at Upton Grey was designed by Gertrude Jekyll when she was aged 66 between November 1908 and April 1909. In their book *Gertrude Jekyll; Essays on the Life of a Working Gardener*, Professor Michael Tooley and Primrose Arnander list fifteen gardens that were planned in 1908 and 1909, among which Runton Old Hall, Ashwell Bury House and Hestercombe are particularly important. This list proves Miss Jekyll's astonishing ability to take on several large and demanding commissions at once, and that at a time when copying machines did not exist, transport was slow and private secretaries were rare. Despite this, Upton Grey in its scale, variety and continuity is an important garden both historically and artistically.

The garden stands on sloping land of just under five acres, and the house, with its 15th century foundations, stands in the centre. The soil is alkaline with a pH of between 7 and 8.

A pictorial walk through the garden, in any season, will illustrate Gertrude Jekyll's art. In the vast majority of cases I have tracked down the species and cultivars she used. Where one is lost I have chosen substitutes as close as possible to her originals. That selection of her plants may explain why, one hundred years ago, herbaceous borders could prove more demanding to manage than today. Modern cultivars occasionally, but by no means always, are more disease-resistant and they are often bred to be more compact or more upright, in other words more manageable. As I follow Miss Jekyll's plans as strictly as possible, I am grateful that today's mechanical devices can increase efficiency and save hours of work.

A gardener who worked here in the 1920s, and who was still alive when we came to Upton Grey in 1984, told me there had once been nine gardeners at the Manor House. He

added, when I said that I managed with one gardener, Philip Brailsford, that there had been a gap in the yew hedge through which they disappeared to the village pub from time to time! It is also possible that the nine gardeners worked in the gardens of two houses. Both were owned by Charles Holme; the other was Upton Grey House, across the road, to which Holme moved while letting the Manor House.

Charles Holme founded the most influential Arts and Crafts magazine of its time, *The Studio*, in 1893 (four years before Edward Hudson founded *Country Life Illustrated*). His eclectic magazine covered design, craft and art in several fields including architecture, jewellery, wrought iron, photography, posters and horticulture. It played an important part in defining crafts as applied or decorative art. John Ruskin, who was convinced that craftsmen deserved status as artists, stated in his lecture The Two Paths: 'Fine art is that in which the hand, the head and the heart of man go together.' That surely applies to gardening as much as to any craft.

In her book *Colour in the Flower Garden*, published by Country Life in 1908, Miss Jekyll explained her belief that gardening deserves to be considered a Fine Art.

'It becomes a point of honour to be always striving for the best. It is just in the way it is done that lies the whole difference between commonplace gardening and gardening that may rightly claim to rank as a fine art.'

From 1889 until 1902 Charles Holme lived at Red House in Bexley Heath, Kent which Philip Webb had designed for William Morris in 1860. During that time Holme's friend

*Portrait of Charles Holme 1848-
1923 by P.A. de Laszlo. Holme, who
founded the Arts & Crafts magazine*
The Studio *in 1893, owned the
Manor House at Upton Grey.*

The Studio, *the leading Arts &
Crafts magazine of its era, was
audacious in employing the
controversial but talented Aubrey
Beardsley to illustrate its first issue.*

Christopher Dresser, who had taught Miss Jekyll at South
Kensington Art School in 1861, introduced him to Japan and
Japanese art and that was to make a lasting impression on him.
Holme joined the Japan Society in 1891, the year of its inception.

In 1902 Holme moved from Red House to the village of
Upton Grey, where he bought several houses and most of the
surrounding farmland. Ernest Newton (1856-1922), a
founder member of the Art Workers' Guild, was the architect
he employed to make what is described at the Royal Institute
of British Architects (RIBA) as 'alterations and additions' to
the Manor House. In 1908, when that work was completed,
Gertrude Jekyll was commissioned to design the surrounding
five-acre garden and field.

There is, however, one perplexing problem. Was it Charles
Holme or his first tenant, a Mr Best, who was responsible for
commissioning Miss Jekyll at Upton Grey?

It was Miss Jekyll's practice to send her clients traced copies
of the plans for their gardens. The originals were kept at
Munstead Wood, which together with most of its contents
was left to her nephew, Francis Jekyll, on her death in 1932.

When the house and some of its contents were sold, the
American landscape architect, Beatrix Farrand, arranged to buy
most of Miss Jekyll's plans, albums and letters. These, together
with a valuable collection of gardening books, Mrs. Farrand
kept at her house, 'Reef Point' in Maine, Massachusetts.

Three years before her death in 1959 Mrs Farrand sent her
collection of horticultural documents to the University of
California, at Berkeley. Those, together with other
horticultural documents, became known as The Reef Point
Collection, named after Mrs Farrand's house in Maine.
When cataloguing the Jekyll documents, Berkeley University
stamped the plans for Upton Grey as having been
commissioned by Mr Best. This was surprising since I have
photographs of Charles Holme and his family in this garden,
which were taken at some point between 1906 and 1908.

Whilst researching at Hampshire Archives in Winchester I
discovered that a Mr Best had indeed occupied the Manor House
as a tenant of Holme's from 1909 to 1915. If Mr Best was simply
a tenant, why did he make such a large investment for a relatively

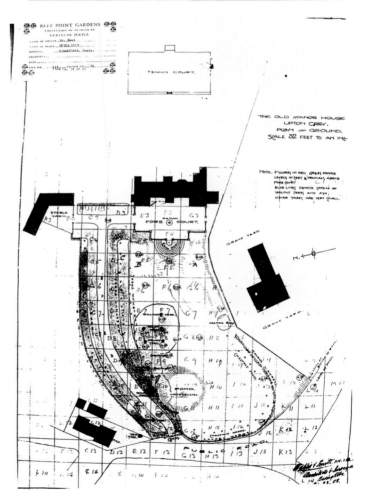

short period? He was extravagant in employing a well-known designer (Jekyll) and he was evidently doing away with the steep grass banks that ran from the house. The work of moving and retaining earth to make terraces would have taken a great deal of time and money and would have been an audacious change.

Knowing Holme's admiration for Japanese art and nature, some of the planting is very suggestive of Holme's influence and when digging near the house I found Japanese Netsuke figures buried in rubble. However we do know that in 1919 a Mrs Best commissioned Miss Jekyll to design her garden at Fawke Wood, near Sevenoaks in Kent. So perhaps a widow or a wealthy family named Best first rented the Manor House and then, impressed with their designer's work, consulted her again on moving to Kent.

One other explanation is that Berkeley University simply relied on information taken from Francis Jekyll's biography of his aunt. That book, entitled *Gertrude Jekyll: a Memoir*, was published in 1934. At the end of his book Francis Jekyll lists most of Miss Jekyll's commissions. Upton Grey is listed under the year 1908 only, although her plans are dated 1908 and 1909. The architects are named as Wallis and Smith. They almost certainly oversaw the work, but it was Ernest Newton who was responsible for the drawings that are now held at The Royal Institute of British Architects in London, and they acknowledge that 'alterations and

additions to The Old Manor House' are by him. Francis gave Ernest Newton no mention; one of several accepted inaccuracies in his book. It was published only two years after his aunt's death. Perhaps that was a little too soon for accurate editing.

If Charles Holme had been responsible for commissioning Gertrude Jekyll to design his garden, it is quite possible that he expected to influence her planting, and this makes me keep an open mind on precisely who did employ her. Within the five acres there is evidence of Holme's admiration for all things Japanese. There are three stands of rampant bamboo in the Wild garden and we found four flowering Japanese cherry trees, each about 70 years old, in the garden. None of those trees was on her plans. In any work of art that has been created on commission, it is probable that the client has had some influence, and this should be remembered when seeing Upton Grey's garden. It is to Miss Jekyll's credit that she probably made a few carefully chosen concessions to her clients – without compromising her art. Bamboos were fashionable at that time and Miss Jekyll often used them in her woodland plans. In the Munstead Wood nursery catalogue she lists *Bambusa Metake* and *Bambusa Simonii* (those names have now changed). They are one of the very few plants on Miss Jekyll's plans that I do not like. Apart from needing constant control, I find them alien in

The Formal Garden today with planted drystone walls. The small wall in the foregound is important in breaking the grass bank between the tennis and bowling lawns. Here Gertrude Jekyll is again designing with an architect's eye, making what she described as 'vertical flower-beds'.

this small wild garden. Charles Holme died in 1923 and is buried in the church-yard a few feet from this garden.

After Mr Best left Upton Grey, the tenancy passed to Mr Walter Henry Savill, brother of Eric Savill, owner of the Savill Gardens in Surrey. Walter Henry Savill took on the lease of the Manor House in 1916. His generous descendants gave me a great many important photographs of the garden which were taken in the early years of the twentieth century and those I have included in the following text.

In 1984 I bought copies of our plans from the University of California at Berkeley, and it is thanks to their care of the plans that we were able to restore the garden so accurately.

Horticultural design, among the most ephemeral of arts, is often the most straightforward to restore. Today Gertrude Jekyll is best remembered for her artistic use of colour, possibly because herbaceous colour is something many gardeners can relate to in today's smaller gardens. In *Colour in the Flower Garden*, published in 1908, she described how to thread colours through the borders in drifts of herbaceous plants and shrubs that run from cool whites and blues to warmer yellows and a crescendo of hot orange and red in the centre. This is evident in Upton Grey's two main borders where old cottage garden favourites, as well as some new plant discoveries, make a magnificent display. Delphinium, helianthus, helenium, rudbeckia, oriental poppies and gladioli are some of the instruments in this crescendo of colour. She also used vividly coloured dahlias and African marigolds in these borders. They, like other features in art, became unfashionable for a time. It is largely thanks to the late Christopher Lloyd at Great Dixter in East Sussex that a great many bright coloured flowers regained popularity. Miss Jekyll wrote of the problem that cycles of fashion can cause in gardening. In *Wood and Garden* she described how a visitor had shown surprise at seeing 'those horrid old bedding plants' in her garden. She defended their use and pointed out that such plants were only 'passive agents in their own misuse.'

Even in this relatively small Edwardian garden at Upton Grey it is evident that Gertrude Jekyll's art was not limited to formal

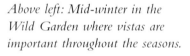

Above left: Mid-winter in the Wild Garden where vistas are important throughout the seasons.

Above right: Autumn colours at the pond. The Wild Garden's colours change quite dramatically with the seasons.

Opposite: Jonathan Myles-Lea's portrait of the entire garden and churchyard.

planting. As you will see, her Wild, or Free-styled gardens were just as important to her. Her art was broad and eclectic.

Comparing gardens of the twenty-first century with those of Miss Jekyll's era demonstrates how fashion in art changes with the economic and social conditions of the day. Today's gardeners prefer styles that are less complicated and labour-intensive with grasses, shrubs, trees and structural themes which form a clean, strong design. They reflect trends towards minimalism in several arts.

Because Miss Jekyll valued plants for their simple, mass effect, she tended to use tested, reliable plants, many of which were those she had seen and loved in the cottage gardens of her beloved Surrey. In *Wood and Garden* she wrote:

'I have learnt much from the little cottage gardens that help to make our English waysides the prettiest in the temperate world.'

She was also an adventurous gardener. In her nursery at Munstead Wood she bred new cultivars, some of which became accepted by the Royal Horticultural Society, from whom she received several awards. When on her travels in Mediterranean countries she bought back plants which she tested for hardiness at Munstead Wood and, if satisfactory, later introduced to the

gardens she was designing. She also used very new cultivars; *Gladiolus* x *brenchleyensis* is one that was introduced but, until recently, was presumed lost until Professor Michael Tooley found and re-introduced it to the gardening world in 2005. One rose, 'Kitchener,' that she used in several gardens, yet which never passed sufficient rigorous tests to reach the general market, is marked on the Upton Grey plans.

It was Gertrude Jekyll's ability to incorporate so many forms of garden art in her commissions that I have learnt to admire most in her work. She was designing gardens at a time when the supporters of the two contrasting styles, 'Formal' and 'Free' were often at odds with each other. Upton Grey's garden demonstrates very clearly how she uses both styles to best effect and it reveals the beauty of both.

In the nineteenth and early twentieth centuries the two leading advocates of those styles were Reginald Blomfield and William Robinson. Blomfield, the architectural gardener, proclaimed formal garden design to be the true art. Straight lines, where herbaceous borders lay among terraces, walls, hedges and pergolas, made for a fine and almost theatrical display of taste; whereas free, natural gardening was, to his supporters, 'vulgar with lines that wriggle.' Blomfield believed that no gardener was capable of planning a garden. 'It is,' he wrote 'the architect's role.'

In the portrait of the garden by Jonathan Myles-Lea (opposite) you can see how the two styles, 'Formal' and 'Free', are used at Upton Grey.

To the south-east of the Manor House lies Miss Jekyll's formal-styled garden. Here there are no curved lines and one part leads to another via steps or pergola, creating different scenes (but not 'rooms' in a structure). Borders are straight-edged but are planted with simple cottage garden plants to soften the effect and to prolong the flowering season. She did not like the severe appearance of the popular Victorian rose gardens which usually held no soft companion planting.

A yew hedge surrounds the planned area, and planted dry-stone walls hold the drop in levels to create the effect of vertical flowerbeds. They replace the earlier heavy grass banks. In *Wall and Water Gardens* Miss Jekyll wrote dismissively of grass banks.

'Hardly anything can be so undesirable in a garden. Such banks are unbeautiful, troublesome to mow, and wasteful of spaces that might be full of interest.'

She was right; in spring and early summer the dry-stone walls are filled with colour and the overall effect of the Formal Garden, in its season, is both spectacular and gentle.

However, Reginald Blomfield's formal gardens of herbaceous flowers and shrubs, laid out in rigid beds, were disparagingly described by the irascible William Robinson as looking like 'colourful tarts on a pastry-cook's tray.' He encouraged gardeners to work with nature using the free, natural or wild style. Simplistically Robinson preferred to wind paths through shrubs, woodland, and natural water where possible, and on into nature.

Because the garden at Upton Grey is narrow, Miss Jekyll put the Wild Garden to the north-west of the house and the Formal style to the south-east. Ideally a Gertrude Jekyll garden would surround the house with formal planting which, like her garden at Munstead Wood, would run gently into managed woodland and nature.

To the north-west of the Manor House, in what was once a field with a naturally spring-fed pond, the Wild Garden is laid out in a completely different style to the Formal. There are no straight lines. She designed the Wild Garden to start with semi-circular grass steps leading to grass paths that meander through first rambling, then species, roses, clusters of wild flowers, to shrubs, a copse of walnut trees, a pond and on into nature. The mood in this side of the garden is very different from the Formal. It is

A Garden designed by Gertrude Jekyll in 1908 ~ Restored by Rosamund Wallinger since 1984

Jonathan Myles-Lea ~ 2006

peaceful, almost graceful, and its beauty runs on through the seasons. Even in mid-winter, when the Formal Garden is virtually bare earth and structure, the grasses, shrubs and trees in the Wild Garden acknowledge the seasons with changing colours and frost-fronded twigs. It has a sophistication that the flamboyant Formal Garden cannot aspire to match.

Miss Jekyll, who was inclined to see 'sermons in stones and good in everything' (of merit) wrote, almost poetically, of the two styles:

'Both are right and both are wrong but the former [formal] are architects to a man. They are limited. They ignore the immense resources that are the precious possession of modern gardeners.... The formalists are unjust when they assume that every path not in a straight line must therefore 'wriggle', and that any shaped or moulded ground must deserve such a term as an 'irrelevant hummock'. Or that, in general, gardening other than formal is 'vulgar'. It is not to be denied that there are wriggles and hummocks and vulgarities in plenty.... But it is unfair to assume that these are in obedience to the principles of the free school. On the contrary, it teaches us to form and respect large quiet spaces of lawn, unbroken by flower beds or any encumbrance; it teaches the simple grouping of noble types of hardy vegetation, whether their beauty be that of flower or foliage or general aspect. It insists on the importance of putting the right thing in the right place, a matter which involves both technical knowledge and artistic ability; it teaches us restraint and

Opposite: The Wild Garden in mid-summer. The planting becomes freer and more natural as it recedes from the house.

The Wild Garden in midwinter.

Aerial photograph of the Formal Garden in 1968. The pergola and Rose garden beds have disappeared and large trees grow in herbaceous borders. Miss Jekyll's garden is almost lost.

proportion in the matter of numbers or quantity, to use enough and not too much of any one thing at a time; to group plants in sequences of good colouring and with due regard to their form and stature and season of blooming, or of autumnal beauty of foliage. It teaches us to study the best means of treatment of different sizes, to see how to join house to garden and garden to woodland.'

The truth of that statement is evident in every part of the garden at Upton Grey.

It is this fundamental open-mindedness to styles and plant material that makes Miss Jekyll's books and gardens so relevant to many of today's gardeners. It was not the fault of the plants, she believed, that they were used in silly and uninteresting ways. She described those artless forms of gardening as 'planting with lowly aspiration,' and she was well aware of the often unsatisfactory influence that fashion had on her clients' choice of plants.

In her first book *Wood and Garden,* published in 1899, Miss

Jekyll demonstrated her love of nature, water, trees and woodland planting, and I believe it was her woodland at Munstead that she most loved. It is difficult to make a valid comparison between the two styles, but I have learnt to love and appreciate the Wild Garden at Upton Grey.

The photographs in this book can assist the reader in deciding whether or not they like a Jekyll garden. There are very few parts of the garden that I find hard to appreciate, and many more that I find quite breath-taking in their seasons. There are certainly plants and combinations of planting that I would not use today for purely practical reasons, but which I do, precisely as the 1908 plans prescribe, in order to demonstrate the restrictions and fashions of that time.

Her obituary in *The Times*, December 1932, credited her with 'not only the complete transformation of English horticultural method and design, but also that wide diffusion of knowledge and taste that has made us almost a nation of gardeners.'

The First World War from 1914 to 1918 made an impact on gardens. Young men were called up, labour was scarce and employers were asked to economise where possible. Miss Jekyll was typical in turning some of her beloved borders to food crops and, apparently, allowed chickens to run freely in her garden. For at least four years gardening as leisure and art was severely curtailed. In a great many cases the hands that worked the gardens were sent from their picturesque acres, across the English Channel, to the bloody, godless trenches that brutalised both man and nature.

After the war a poorer Europe continued to abandon demanding gardens, and the Great Depression that preceded World War II accelerated the decline in horticulture.

Like thousands of other gardens, Upton Grey's glory as a fine garden passed into less affluent, more practical hands, until the early 1980's when we found it derelict and overgrown.

Wandering through the Manor House's garden today you can pepper your journey with Jekyll's familiar and apposite dictums. She described filling the ground with plants as being as poetry is to words, the best use in the best context and, as I have mentioned, painting the landscape with living things. In the Wild

The Formal Garden from the tennis lawn as we found it in 1984.

Garden she advised 'liberty but not license' and that the woodland should not be 'tormented'. Her books are beautifully written and they continue to inspire and educate today's gardeners. She believed that with a little learning anyone could make their own garden a place of art. As Horace Walpole wisely wrote:

The Wild Garden in 1984. The leaden cherubs had been removed from the entrance gates and large trees, ivy and brambles had grown throughout.

'In general it is probably true that the Possessor, if he has any taste, must be the best designer of his own improvements. He sees his situation in all seasons of the year, at all times of the day. He knows where beauty will not clash with convenience and observes in his silent walks or accidental rides a thousand hints that must escape a person who in a few days sketches out a pretty picture but has not the leisure to examine the details and relations of every part.'

CHAPTER TWO

The Rose Garden

'One may learn from Nature these great lessons, the importance of moderation, of reserve, of simplicity of intention'
Wood and Garden

Opposite: The pergola, Rose Garden and Formal Garden from the house. The hundred-year-old Formal Garden is now completely restored.

The Rose Garden is set in the centre of the Formal Garden. Miss Jekyll's 1908 plans show it as straight-edged and geometric in structure. The fashion in garden design of that era had been to surround the house with geometric outlines which resulted in a formal garden where planting was often as rigid as the design. As Miss Jekyll was working for a client it is probable that she was asked to include the very popular rose garden in her plans.

In *Garden Ornament,* published by Country Life in 1918, she wrote,

'We are growing impatient of the usual Rose garden, generally a sort of target of concentric rings of beds placed upon turf, often with no special aim at connected design with the portions of the garden immediately about it, and filled with plants without any thought of their colour effect or any other worthy intention.'

In that sentence she emphasises the important point that garden art should balance both with its surrounding architecture and with nature. That is an element of garden design that I find is often overlooked today. And in *Wood and Garden* she described such gardening as being 'so cheap of mental effort.'

At Upton Grey you can see how Miss Jekyll's skilful use of what have come to be known as cottage garden plants, among the roses and canna, softens the effect and adds colour and scent to the area. This is far more interesting than the standard, rather sterile, Victorian rose gardens that featured roses only.

'Planting is to gardens as poetry is to words; the best use in the best context.'

The Formal Garden at Upton Grey is surrounded by planted dry-stone walls on three sides, and these give an extended season to the area's flowers; to Miss Jekyll they acted as vertical flowerbeds. On the south-facing sides the walls hold rock and alpine plants that flourish in the warm, dry days of March and April.

The north-facing wall is planted with hartstongue fern [*Phyllitis scolopendrium*] and small shade-tolerant plants that include *Cardamine pratensis* and *Corydalis ochroleuca*. Because it is cooler, that wall has a longer flowering season than the other two walls.

Later, in May, most of the colour and drama moves from the walls to the four trapezoidal beds that surround the central stone squares. Here China roses, Hybrid Tea and Tea roses, that flower intermittently from now until the frosts of winter, are grown among peonies, lilies and an edging of stachys. Miss Jekyll described this planting in *Roses for English Gardens*, written with Edward Mawley and published by Country Life in 1901:

The formal and free ways should both be used. The two are always best when brought into harmonious companionship.'

Looking carefully at Miss Jekyll's plant list for the Rose Garden (see page 27) she lists eight yellow Cassinia at six shillings. This is followed by eight and two of plants whose names are very hard to decipher. The first looks a little like Funkia grandiflora [*Hosta plantaginea* var. *grandiflora*]. On her plan she simply wrote 'plant', short for plantain, so I suspect that is probably correct. The second I cannot begin to make out. It may be 'green canna.' Those plants certainly do appear in the two stone squares, but having no definitive transcription, I used purple-leafed canna.

There is no doubt that this area of the garden is sensational in its season, but that season is limited to spring and summer.

Looking eastward over the Rose Garden in late June. The later-flowering lactiflora peonies 'Sarah Bernhardt' have taken over from the earlier-flowering officinalis peonies 'Lize van Veen', thus extending their colourful season.

Other parts of the garden take on the display during high autumn and winter.

Keeping the roses in the Rose Garden healthy is an annual struggle. Each trapezoidal bed holds nine peonies, eight roses, seventeen lilies and fifty-five *Stachys lanata* [*S. byzantina*]. Peonies,

both *P.officinalis* and *P.lactiflora*, grow luxuriantly at the expense of the roses, although all are fed regularly and mulched bi-annually.

Because Miss Jekyll did not specify which peonies were to be used it was essential that we chose only from those available before 1908. I selected one that flowers early; from

late April in some years. It is quite a rare peony, an officinalis, named 'Lize van Veen'. The other is a later flowering lactiflora peony, the splendid 'Sarah Bernhardt' which flowers from early June well into July. For continued flowering and balance we have planted some of both in each bed. The impact of the peonies when in flower is quite breathtaking.

Between the peonies Miss Jekyll's five roses struggle to make any effective display, particularly the three Hybrid Teas. It is probable that Miss Jekyll preferred the older, tried and trusted roses to the new, rather demanding, species, but when she designed this garden in 1908, rose gardens were the height of fashion and the new Hybrid Tea roses, the first of which 'La

The Rose Garden looking westward in June. It lies at a lower level to the main herbaceous borders at each side, and can be seen from the paths that run at the top of the dry-stone walls.

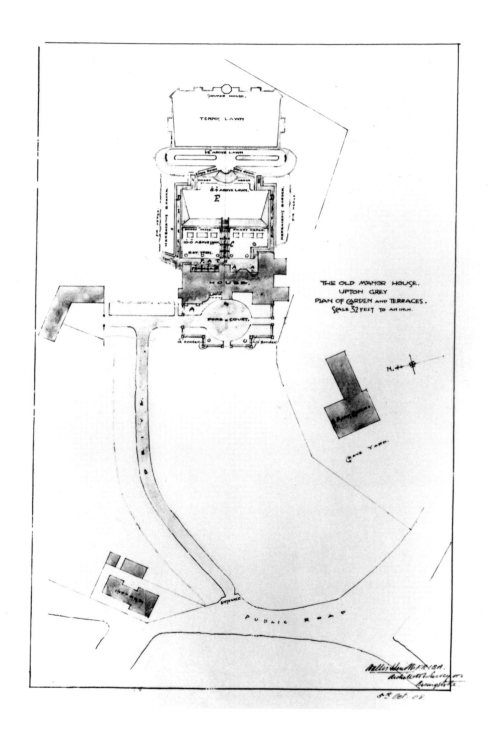

THE OLD MANOR HOUSE.
UPTON GREY
PLAN OF GARDEN AND TERRACES.
SCALE 32 FEET TO AN INCH.

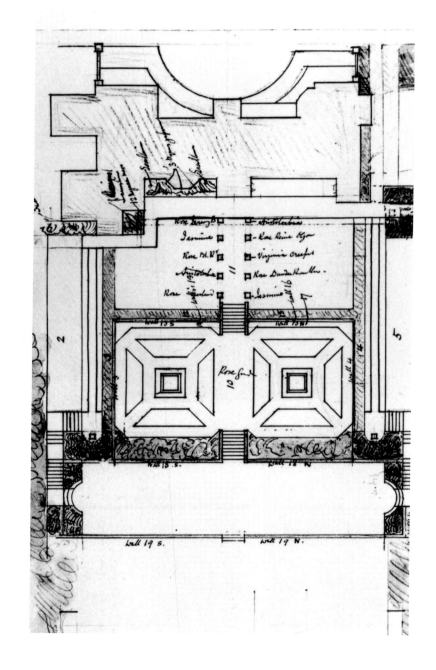

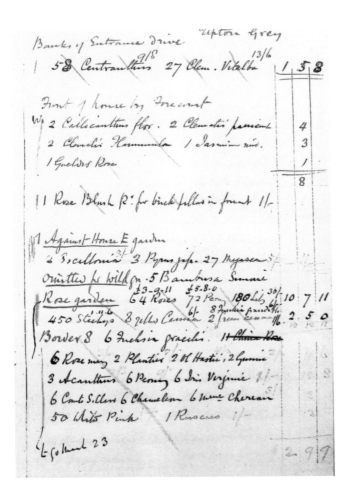

France' was bred by Guillot in France in 1865, were in great demand. Richard Bisgrove, an acknowledged authority on Gertrude Jekyll, wrote 'She rarely, if ever, used roses in the conventional Victorian way in a Rose garden. She desired a more natural look. She acknowledged the troubles she had with the new Hybrid Teas.'

In these rose beds the three Hybrid Teas are 'Madame Caroline Testout' (Pernet-Ducher, France 1890) which was only available as a climber in England in the early 1980s, 'Madame Abel Chatenay' (Pernet-Ducher, France 1895) and the third is 'Killarney.' I spent the first eight years at Upton Grey searching for that very rare

Hybrid Tea rose. In 1992 Hazel Le Rougetel introduced me to the important Italian rosarian Professor Fineschi and the following year he generously sent me three rooted cuttings of 'Killarney' from his famous rose garden in Umbria. None of the Hybrid Teas likes our thin chalky soil and 'Madame Caroline Testout' particularly dislikes being cut down to an unnatural shrub shape several times a year. In 1998 I finally managed to buy the shrub form from the French rosarian André Eve.

There are two other roses on the plan. One is a China Rose, 'Madame Laurette Messiny' (Guillot, France 1887)

Left: Munstead Wood nursery's plant list for the Rose Garden. These were written by Miss Jekyll and show the impressive amount of plants that she was able to provide for her many commissions.

Above: Rose 'Mme Caroline Testout' (H.T. 1890).

Opposite left: The surveyor's plan of the Formal Garden showing the massive grass banks that Gertrude Jekyll converted into planted dry-stone walls.

Opposite right: Gertrude Jekyll's plan for the centre of the Rose Garden.

Paeonia lactiflora 'Sarah Bernhardt'. A strong, reliable and late-flowering peony.

Paeonia officinalis 'Lize van Veen'.

Rose 'Killarney' (H.T.) 1898.

Stachys lanata [S. byzantina].

Rose 'Mme Lombard' (Tea) 1878.

and the other, 'Madame Lombard' (Lacharme, France 1878) is a Tea Rose. All five need care and extra feeding, particularly when the voracious and strong peonies are in full growth.

After twenty-four years of struggle and irritation with the perfidious hybrid teas I introduced six of the David Austin New English Rose 'Eglantine' to the Rose Garden. It is a strong, pretty and long-flowering rose which is putting its neighbours to shame. I suppose in any relationship a constant struggle to please exhausts patience. Mine is on the ebb. With

some effort we can now get a recurrent flowering from the various roses which starts in May and carries on until the frosts. Future gardeners here can return to Miss Jekyll's choices as they will still be available, if only in other parts of the world. I am told by a friend that if a rose is bred north of where it grows it should flourish. So far I have not disproved that theory.

As peony 'Sarah Bernhardt' begins to lose its flowers, a finely scented white lily comes into bloom. In this case I was advised not to rely on Miss Jekyll's choice and this is one of the very few

Left: Rose 'Mme Abel Chatenay' (H.T.) 1895.

Right: Rose 'Mme Laurette Messimy' (China) 1887.

Above left: One Rose Garden bed with Paeonia lactiflora 'Sarah Bernhardt' in flower, June.

Left: One Rose Garden bed with Lilium regale in flower, July.

Above right: Lilium regale surrounding one of the central stone squares in the Rose Garden. Grown in this enclosed area means that throughout most of the summer the Rose Garden is filled with scents of peonies and lilies.

Opposite: One of the central Purbeck stone squares in the Rose Garden. Lilies in pots and Canna indica will take over the flowering successionally throughout most of the summer.

exceptions that I have made to her plans, so I have used *Lilium regale* instead of *Lilium longiflorum*. *L. longiflorum* is very rarely winter hardy and requires a great deal of work and attention. *L. regale* was introduced in 1903 by Dr. E. H. 'Chinese' Wilson and it has been justifiably popular ever since. Its scent fills the Rose Garden from June to late July.

Each bed is edged with a border of *Stachys lanata* [*S. byzantina*]. With the exception of the lilies we have used Miss Jekyll's cultivars whenever they are still available. *Stachys lanata* is not as good a shape as modern varieties. It grows tall and leggy and, as Miss Jekyll advised, we have to remove flowers and trim it several times a year to keep it compact. But this garden is planted to demonstrate the challenges as well as the virtues of a one hundred year old garden.

Below left: Lilium regale and young Canna indica leaves in July.

Above centre: Canna indica in flower.

Below centre: Un-trimmed Stachys lanata – looking 'leggy'.

Right: Canna indica in one of the central stone squares in October.

Opposite: Flowers of Lilium regale *whose fine scent fills the Rose garden in mid-summer.*

THE CENTRAL RAISED SQUARE STONE BEDS
'Groups of tall cannas where I want grand foliage.'
Wood and Garden

In the centre of each side of the Rose garden the stone squares hold *Canna indica* and more regale lilies. The cannas make a dramatic late summer display with their strong, dark, purple–green leaves and orange flowers. This plant, although it looks exotic, has been used in English gardens for a surprisingly long time. It was introduced to Europe from Central America via Africa in about 1565. It is sometimes known as Indian Shot, possibly because its very hard seeds were once used as pellets.

The cannas are the last plants to flower in the Rose Garden, so extending that area's season into late autumn and the first frosts. But they are not hardy in this garden, and we bring the plants in each winter. I am told that in sheltered areas they may survive in the ground under protective covering.

BORDERS 8 AND 9

'Every year, as I gain more experience and, I hope more powers of critical judgement, I find myself tending towards broader and simpler effects, both of grouping and colour.'

The two larger borders in the Rose Garden, Borders 8 and 9 on her plans, are filled mainly with shrubs. These enclose the area to the south east and they act as a wind break. The shrubs here include China roses as well as *Olearia x haastii* and *Olearia phlogopappa*; the latter known to Miss Jekyll as *Olearia gunnii*.

A cross on her plan simply marks where a China rose should be planted, so I chose three that were available before 1908. They are *Rosa* 'Hermosa' (1840), *Rosa* 'Cecile Brunner' (1881) and *Rosa* 'Duke of York' (1894).

This area holds relatively little colour. The larger plants and shrubs in both these borders and the walls under them are predominantly green and grey; there are few flowers and their colours are soft. Miss Jekyll wrote of the value of these peaceful areas in a garden, and of their beauty throughout the seasons when herbaceous flowers were over. She described how, when planning and planting an area she might walk through holding proposed plants before deciding exactly where to put them.

Today's gardeners make more use of shrubs in borders. They are considerably easier to manage than herbaceous plants. Even if deciduous, shrubs provide shape throughout the year. Rather fewer of them can run uncontrollably through the borders and very few need careful staking.

Above: From the Tennis Lawn to the house early July showing borders 8 and 9 from beneath.

Opposite: Towards Borders 9 and 8 from the raised path that edges the Rose Garden. May. Miss Jekyll wrote of the importance of grey and silver foliage.

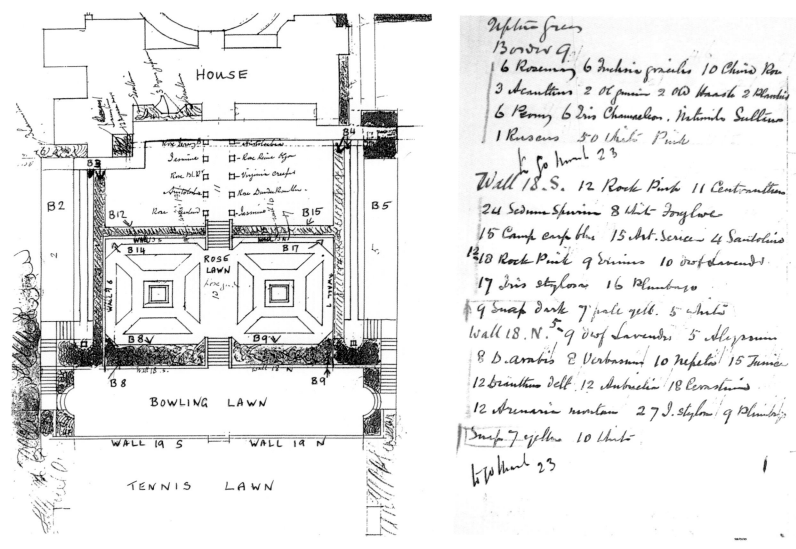

Above left: Gertrude Jekyll's plan for the Formal Garden.

Above right: Munstead Wood nursery's list includes plants for Border 9.

Opposite: Overlooking Border 8 in July.

Most require clipping into shape but I find that a small price to pay for such helpful behaviour.

Five *Fuchsia magellanica* var. *gracilis* fill the centre at the back of both borders. In late summer and autumn their branches hang prettily over the dry-stone wall at their feet. Between these grow large plants, shrub-like in shape, *Acanthus spinosus*, and peonies. Along the top of the wall, between the fuchsias, grow *Santolina chamaecyparissus* and *Santolina incana*. At the ends of the beds the evergreen shrubs *Rosmarinus officinalis* and *Ruscus racemosus* [*Danae racemosa*] grow, to balance and round off the borders. Smaller plants, hostas (here Miss Jekyll has written 'plant', short for 'plantain', on the plan), then dianthus and *Iris germanica,* grow along the front edges. These two borders, unlike the main herbaceous borders, maintain shape and some interest throughout the year.

Looking towards the rose arbour from between Borders 8 and 9. Here the steps down to the bowling lawn are edged with rosemary and lavender. Miss Jekyll often lined steps and paths with sweet-smelling plants to brush against by passers-by.

Above: Iris germanica 'Argus Pheasant'. This is one of the very few old varieties of Iris germanica that I was able to track down.

Right: Gertrude Jekyll's plan for Border 8.

Opposite: Overlooking Border 9 in early May. This and Border 8 are the only borders that are largely shrub-filled. With the exception of yucca, olearias and edging plants the rest of the Formal Garden planting dies back to brown earth in mid-winter.

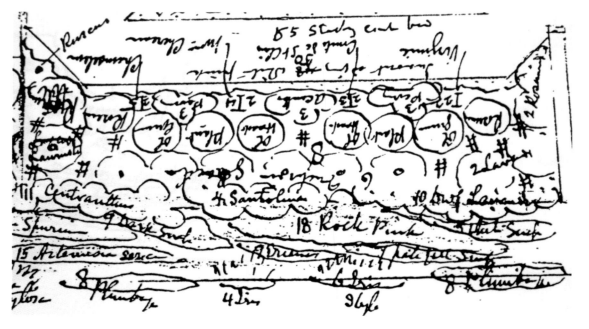

Above left: Acanthus spinosus. This is one of the few plants that had survived from the 1909 garden. It is predictably hard to control – but structurally beautiful.
Above right: Rosa 'Hermosa' (China) 1840.
Below left: Fuchsia magellanica gracilis.
Below right: Gertrude Jekyll's plan for Border 9.

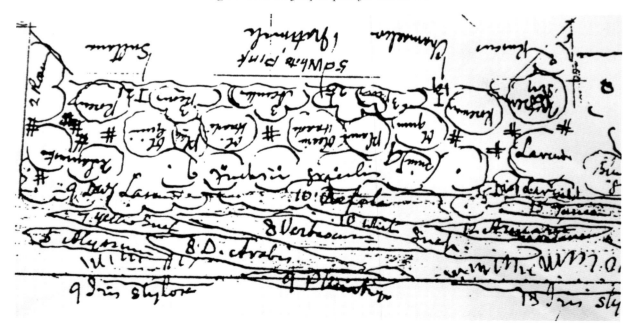

Olearia gunnii [O. phlogopappa]. An evergreen shrub, bloom-covered in May but not always winter hardy. Below: Olearia hastii.

Shallow steps leading to bowling lawn beneath borders 8 and 9 June. Where ever possible Miss Jekyll designed shallow steps for easier access with wheelbarrows, and for visual appeal.
Below left: Rosa 'Cecile Brunner' (China) 1881.
Below centre: Rosa 'Duke of York' (China) 1894.
Below right: Ruscus racemosus, an attractive, shiny-leaved, evergreen shrub that is easy to grow in nearly any situation.

BORDERS 14 AND 17

'I never tire of admiring and praising Iris stylosa. Lovely in form and colour, sweetly scented and with admirable foliage, it has in addition to these merits the unusual one of a blooming season of six months' duration. The first flowers come with the earliest days of November, and its season ends with a rush of bloom in the first half of April.' Wood and Garden

These are two narrow beds that lie at the footing of south-east facing walls on the Rose Garden. At the base of the steps that lead from the pergola on the top terrace into the Rose Garden grow two *Rosmarinus officinalis*. Miss Jekyll often edged paths and steps with sweet-smelling plants and in this garden most pathways hold rosemary, lavender or other scented plants positioned to brush against the passer-by.

Border 15 above Wall 16 with Border 17 footing in late May.

Opposite: Border 12 above Wall 13 and Border 14 at the footing also in early summer.

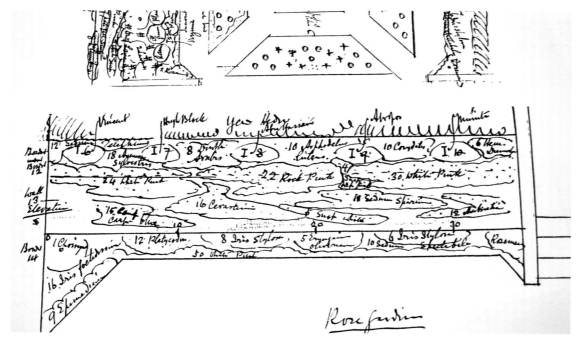

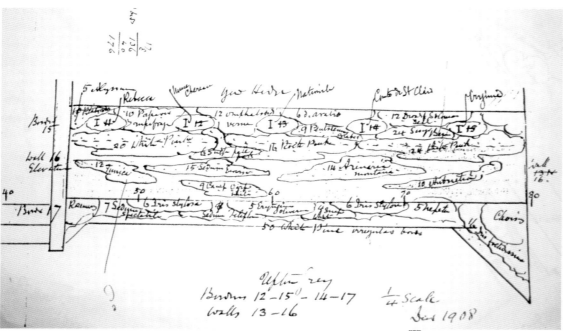

Beside the rosemary grow *Sedum spectabile* and *Iris stylosa* [*I. unguicularis*]. In Border 17 these are followed by *Eryngium oliverianum*, white antirrhinum, more iris and *Nepeta mussinii* [*Nepeta faassenii*]. The corners at the end of each border are filled with *Choisya ternata* under-planted with *Iris foetidissima* and *Epimedium x versicolor 'Sulphureum'*.

The end of Border 14, where it runs into the corner planting, is planted with *Platycodon mariesii*. That valuable, blue or white-flowered plant is at its best in late summer and it is easily grown from seed.

Both borders are edged with dianthus, which are marked 'white pinks' on the plan. I am fairly certain that our *Dianthus caesius* [*D. gratianopolitanus*] and *D. petraeus* and *D. deltoides* have cross-pollinated over the years. They are promiscuous plants but the results are pretty and very similar to Miss Jekyll's pinks.

Eryngium oliverianum. The vivid blue of this plant lights up a border.

Iris stylosa [I. unguicularis]. This plant likes a hot dry position in poor soil.

Rosmarinus officinalis. A wonderful plant for attracting bees.

Far right: Sedum spectabile. Another plant that is loved by insects.

*Far left: Antirrhinum
white.*

*Below left: Nepeta
mussinii
[N. x faassenii].*

Left: Iris foetidissima.

*Below: Platycodon
mariessii.*

Right: Epimedium x versicolour 'Sulphureum'.

Far right: Choisya ternata.

Below left: Dianthus mixed cultivar pink.

Below right: Dianthus mixed cultivar white. Dianthus derives from the Greek 'dios' and anthus 'flower of the gods' a name used by Theophrastus, so evidently a plant that has been popular for centuries. It is a large genus with over 300 species.

BORDERS 12 AND 15
'All good gardening has its foundation in common sense'

These two narrow borders, each 90 cm wide, run along the tops of the dry-stone walls that enclose the south-east facing side of the rose garden. The soil is thin, chalky and very rarely enriched with compost. The plants here evidently enjoy these spartan conditions.

Before Miss Jekyll was commissioned to design the garden Charles Holme had started work on its structure. Steep grass banks were built to run down from the house towards the village, and along the edge of the top terrace a yew hedge had been planted. Although Miss Jekyll had accepted the yew on her plans it is quite impractical as yew grows vigorously in this chalky Hampshire soil. Within a few years there would have been no room for the narrow border at its roots. So with professional advice we changed that hedge to the smaller, more controllable box. Today *Buxus sempervirens* divides the bed from the grass terrace and its height is limited to 40 cm. That allows space and light for the early flowering plants in the beds beyond to grow freely.

Above: Border 15, to right of the pergola, in early June.

Opposite: Borders 12 and 15 above the drystone walls. This area is most spectacular in June. It was in this month that the late Geoff Hamilton described my garden as 'a Paradise on Earth'.

A pergola and steps to the Rose Garden divide the two borders. From the easterly side of the pergola, in Border 15, plants run towards Border 4 as follows. First there is an Alyssum; I use *A. saxatile* [*Aurinia saxatilis*]. Several bearded irises, both *I. pallida* and *I. germanica* are spaced along this border. I have not been able to find any of the iris cultivars selected by Miss Jekyll, so have chosen substitutes as close as possible to her originals. *Papaver rupifragrum* run towards *Omphalodes verna*. The omphalodes is from the borage family and grows well as a low ground cover with bright blue flowers in early summer. The papaver have pretty double and single orange flowers and are easily grown from seed. These are followed by dianthus and *Penstemon glaber*. When we started restoring this border only one place in England was listed as growing that fine, winter-hardy and rather delicately shaped penstemon; that was John Coke at his nursery in Bentley, Hampshire. Today it is more readily available. Dwarf Solomon's Seal [*Polygonatum multiflorum*] and antirrhinum run to the corner where this border joins Border 4 at a large shrubby clematis, *Clematis heracleifolia* var. *davidiana*.

An extract from Munstead Wood nursery's plant list for border 15.

Gertrude Jekyll's plan for Border 15.

Opposite: A close view of Border 15 that runs beside a box [Buxus sempervirens] hedge in June.

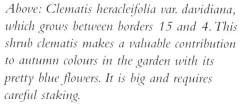

Above: Clematis heracleifolia var. davidiana, which grows between borders 15 and 4. This shrub clematis makes a valuable contribution to autumn colours in the garden with its pretty blue flowers. It is big and requires careful staking.

Above centre: Polygonatum multiflorum sometimes known as Solomon's Seal. This plant provides good green foliage throughout the summer. It is very popular with a local caterpillar and can be eaten to the ground if I am not vigilant.

Above right: Penstemon glaber. This is one of the strong, winter-hardy penstemons, and well worth growing.

Right: Alyssum [Aurinaria saxitalis] The name derives from the Greek 'a' without and 'Lysa' meaning rage, for allaying anger and perhaps rabies. Proof that old Greek's and old wives' tales were not always reliable – it doesn't do much to ease my grumps either.

Above left: Iris germanica, blue. These, like any flower that stands unsupported in a strong wind, are valuable in a border. It has the added virtue of a sweet smell and beautiful flower.

Above right: Iris germanica, mixed colours. The range of colour in this iris species is wide and often spectacular.

Far left: Omphalodes verna is such a vivid blue flower in clear lime-green leaves. It joyously announces the start of spring.

Right: Papaver rupifragrum. A simple, easy, moderately self-seeding little flower, but it has no scent at all.

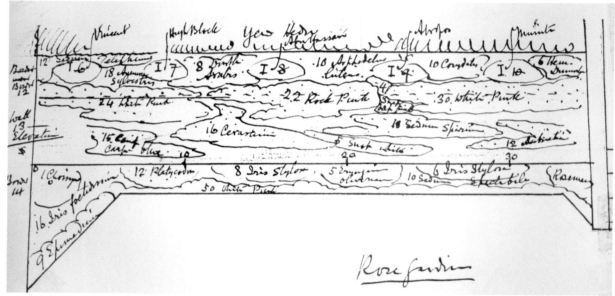

On the other side of the steps Border 12 contains, one of my favourite flowers, the very pretty and sweet smelling *Hemerocallis dumortieri*. The name derives from the Greek, 'Hemere' meaning day and 'Kallos' meaning beauty because most hemerocallis flower for a very short time, but dumortieri flowers are not quite so ephemeral. Visitors are often surprised that this species of day lily has any scent at all. It also has good linear, basal leaves amongst which, when I eventually cut them back at the end of the year, I often find nests of small bantam eggs. This is followed by corydalis, *Asphodeline lutea*, double arabis, and *Anemone sylvestris*. On the Jekyll plans *Sedum telephium* leads to the corner where the bed joins Border 3 at *Olearia haastii*. In 1985 I bought seeds of *Sedum telephium* which, today, is known as Hylotelephium. Dianthus and bearded iris are dotted between those plants along the border.

Above: Asphodeline lutea flower.

Opposite above left: Anemone sylvestris.

Opposite below left: Sedum telephium [Hylotelephium].

Opposite above right: Hemerocallis dumortieri. A very popular and early-flowering day lily with a pleasant scent.

Opposite below right: Arabis caucasica.

Asphodeline lutea group. Rather ungratefully I told a visitor, Mrs Pumfrey, a fine gardener who had given me the plant, that I found these flowers die untidily. 'Nonsense' she replied, 'they are like little night stars that take it in turn to twinkle and fade.' She is right; it has enchantment.

CHAPTER THREE

The Drystone Walls

'One of the best and simplest ways of growing rock-plants is in a loose wall. In many gardens the abrupt change of level makes a retaining wall necessary but when I see this built in the usual way as a solid structure of brick and mortar I regret that it is not built as a home for rock-plants....just what most alpines delight in.'
Wood and Garden

Opposite: The house viewed from the tennis lawn in winter snow.

Below: Purbeck drystone walls under the Rose Garden in July.

Gertrude Jekyll used drystone walls in most of the gardens that lay on sloping land. She disliked heavy grass banks because they presented problems with mowing, and because they provided no ornament. Here her drystone walls prolong the flowering season in the Formal Garden because plants that grow in warm, south-facing walls flower early and freely, before much of the main garden has come into bloom.

Upton Grey's Rose Garden is surrounded on three sides by planted walls that are made with the Purbeck stone whose quarries run from the eastern edge of Dorset coast's Jurassic World Heritage Site. Although the shallow quarries are found within a ten mile square, the colour of the stone varies quite noticeably in different quarries.

Today supplies of Purbeck stone are limited and expensive. We were lucky to find enough remaining from derelict walls to rebuild all with very little need to buy extra stone.

WALLS 13 AND 16

These two south-east facing walls stand under Borders 12 and 15. Nearly all the plants here flower early in the season, giving the effect of vertical flowerbeds until the peonies and roses in the Rose Garden below take over the colour displays. The movement of colour from area to area throughout the season was an element of good design that Gertrude Jekyll was well aware of, and which she described in her articles and books.

The plants she uses in Wall 16 are *Tunica saxifraga [Petrorhagia saxifraga], Sedum ewersii [Hylotelephium ewersii],* white *Campanula carpatica, Arenaria montana* and aubrieta.

Antirrhinum and dianthus grow in and along the top of the wall. The colours are pale and the flowers delicate. The leaves of the sedum, which are sometimes known as stonecrops, are almost as picturesque as the flowers, and as they are evergreen the season is extended throughout the year.

Control of plants in the walls is demanding. My efforts to plant in the dry, dusty cracks in the walls usually fail. When the walls were first built it was simple to fill gaps as walls went up. Today the soil has tumbled out. Weeding pulls out as much earth as weed, and mice have made a complete apartment block of the structure, so parts of the walls are virtually hollow behind.

Right: Munstead Wood nursery's plant list for Wall 16.

Far right: Munstead Wood nursery's plant list for Wall 13.

Below left: Armeria maritma, an easy sun-loving species suited to most garden situations that have good drainage.

Below right: Aubrieta deltoidea named after the botanic artist Claude Aubriet who accompanied Joseph Tournefort on his botanical travels. Both men were killed in Paris in 1706 when hit by a swerving carriage.

*Above left: Tunica saxifraga
[Petrorhagia saxifraga]. A delicate-
looking, delightful plant that enjoys
its position in the drystone walls.*

*Above right: Campanula latifolia
var. macrantha. A favourite of
Miss Jekyll's.*

Left: Arenaria montana flower.

*Right: Sedum ewersii
[Hylotelephium ewersii].*

Opposite: In May Wall 13 is filled with early summer flowers and Cerastium tomentosum, which dominates and needs regular controlling. Now is the time to trim the box hedge.

Right: Antirrhinum in mixed colours. Over the years my cultivars have become thoroughly mixed. If I take my own seeds too often the resulting flowers become weak, so I buy seeds every other year.

Far right: Sedum spurium with Pterocephalus parnassii.

Below left: Sedum spurium.

Below right: A close-up view of Cerastium tomentosum. This plant is known as Snow-in-Summer. Because of its invasive habit it would perhaps be better known as Avalanche in Summer.

Several years after building and planting the walls I find that plants here have a will of their own. They set seed where they feel comfortable and where they do not, they will not grow. Because the colour and shape of the planting is similar, I have given up the yearly destruction of unruly progeny and allow nature to perform as it thinks fit. But when, as they surely will need to be, the walls are rebuilt, I shall have all the correct plants and will return them to their planned places.

Wall 13 is planted with aubrieta, *Sedum spurium*, dianthus and antirrhinum, a blue *Campanula carpatica* and the very invasive *Cerastium tomentosum*, which is sometimes known as Snow-in-Summer. I do control that cerastium because, left untended, it would happily cover the entire wall and most of the surrounding beds.

Above: Phillitis [Asplenium] scolopendrium. [Hartstongue fern].

Opposite: The Purbeck drystone wall under Border 3 in July.

WALL UNDER BORDER 3

'There are, in gardening, more ways of getting into trouble than in any other kind of ornamental art.'

This wall faces north–east and gets little sun, so plants here must be shade tolerant. They include the Hartstongue fern *(Phillitis [Asplenium) scolopendrium]* and corydalis. One of the very few plants that I found in more or less the correct place when we came here in 1984 was *Corydalis ochroleuca*. As we had to dismantle and completely rebuild the virtually derelict walls I kept a few rooted pieces of that plant in holding beds in the kitchen garden. This is a pretty, very pale yellow corydalis that flowers for a long period. It is popular with visitors but I am told that in parts of America it is considered almost a weed.

It is evident that Miss Jekyll's walls include a rather unconventional selection of plants, besides the accepted 'rock

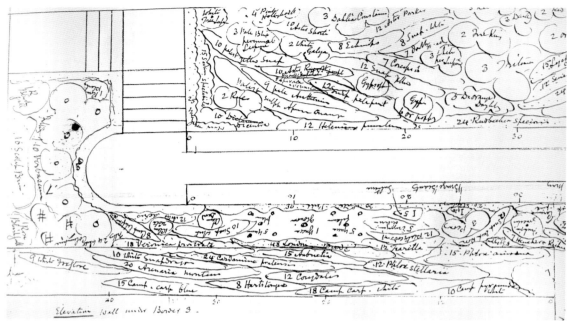

plants.' She had noticed that antirrhinum, small artemisia, asplenium, foxglove and *Erinus alpinus* also thrive in sunny positions where their roots enjoy good drainage. She describes the upright habit they adopt as they lean into the walls as standing like soldiers on sentry duty.

Other plants that grow in this wall are *Arenaria montana*, *Cardamine pratensis*, *Campanula carpatica*, both white and blue, antirrhinums and two phlox, *Phlox Stellaria [P. bifida]* and *Phlox amoena [P. x procumbens]*. At the foot of the wall are white foxgloves (despite being white they are *Digitalis purpurea*) and *Campanula pyramidalis*, in my opinion a much underrated plant. It grows up to 130cm tall and in late summer its stem is covered with strong blue, bell-shaped flowers. It is easy to grow from seed.

Cardamine pratensis means 'of the fields'. This cardamine is not very happy growing in our (now rather hollow) wall; it is far happier growing in the orchard where, although not on the plans, it is doing its own independent thing.

Above: Cardamine pratensis flower. I cannot grow this where Miss Jekyll suggests although it thrives in the orchard where wildflowers grow.

Below: Campanula carpatica white. This is a very useful plant on drystone walls.

Right: The wall under Border 3 in June.

WALL UNDER BORDER 4

'She has a reverence for colour. A clear, logical brain.'
Vita Sackville-West of Gertrude Jekyll.

This drystone wall stands opposite the wall under Border 3. It faces south-west, so the flowering season here is early and quite short. *Pterocephalus parnassii [P. perennis]* is a one of my favourite wall plants. It has pale pink, scabrous-like flower heads and light, feathery seed heads above rounded grey-green tufts of small leaves. It loves this well-drained position in full sunlight. Beside and slightly above that grows *Sedum spurium*. Its chubby rounded leaves look like small reddish pebbles, and its flowers are gentle pink. Dianthus and thrift [*Armeria maritima*] run towards dwarf lavender and aubrieta. A large grouping of nepeta drifts between another group of *Armeria maritima*. Rather surprisingly Miss Jekyll calls this group dwarf thrift, but as far as I know they are one and the same. Bright blue *Lithospermum rosmarinifolia* grow above *Phlox Nelsonii*, and then rock pinks, white foxgloves and verbascum fill the wall to its end above Border 9.

Above: Digitalis purpurea. (White foxglove).

Right: Verbascum lychnitis. Like most verbascums these are structural plants. They grow like columns in architecture.

Far right: Lithospermum rosmarinifolia. A very good ground-cover plant.

Opposite: Wall under Border 4 and surrounding borders in June, when the Formal Garden is at its most splendid.

Gertrude Jekyll's plan for 'wall under border 4'.

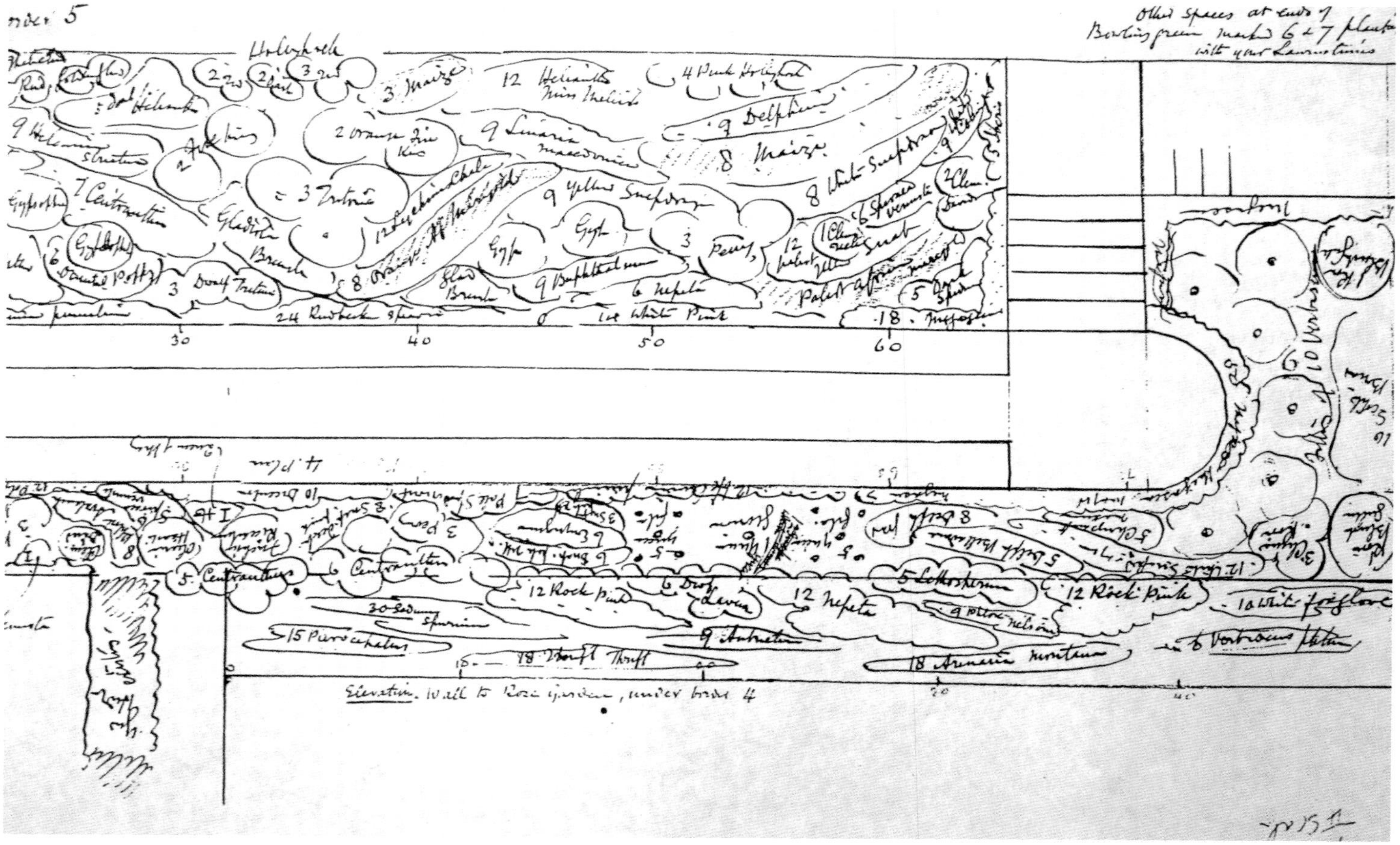

Close-up of Pterocephalus parnassii in flower.

Opposite above left: Pterocephalus parnassii [P. perennis]. There was a surge of interest in 'alpine' and 'rock' plants at the time that Miss Jekyll was designing this garden. Drystone walls provide a good substitute for alpine conditions. This is one of my favourites. It is a little independent, and appears regularly in any place but where intended.

Opposite below left: A corner of the Rose Garden bed showing the edging of Stachys lanata below Paeonia officinalis Lize van Veen.

Opposite far right: Armeria maritima.

I have never quite understood why Miss Jekyll refers to some plants by their botanical names and others by their common name. By 1908 I would have supposed she had established which language to use. I hope this is not heresy, but it certainly confused me as a beginner gardener when I started this restoration.

WALLS 18 SOUTH AND 18 NORTH

"Nothing is prettier or pleasanter than all the various ways of terraced treatment that may be practised with the help of drystone walling.'

The two walls below Borders 8 and 9 overlook the Bowling Lawn. At each end the walls are over three metres high and, because they support such a heavy mass of earth and planting, the stones are mortar-backed, not drystone. Miss Jekyll supplied planting plans for those first few metres of the mortared walls. This could be one reason for believing that Miss Jekyll did not visit the garden. Had she seen the high wall she would have realized that it was impossible to build it without the strengthening cement. However there are a few intentional spaces in the mortar filling. At first I assumed this was a result of aging walls, but they may well have been deliberate. If so, it is likely that the stonemason did not have Miss Jekyll's plan to hand, as there are not as many gaps as intended plants, nor are they in quite the correct places.

Left: Wall 18 south in June. The drystone walls hold plants that flower from February until early summer, so extending the season of colour in those areas.

Opposite: Wall 18 north in early June.

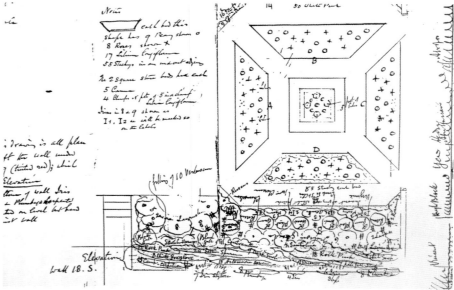

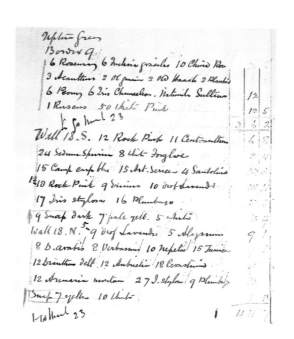

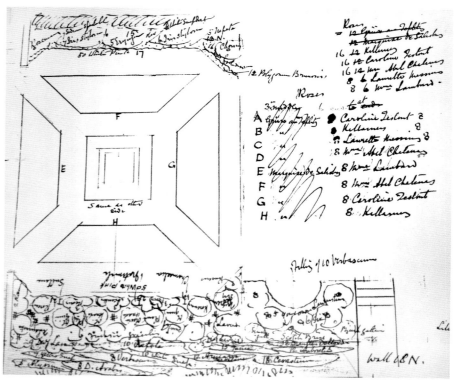

Above: Iris stylosa [I. unguicularis].

Above right: Gertrude Jekyll's plan for Wall 18 south.

Right: Munstead Wood nursery's plant list for Wall 18 south and north.

Far right: Gertrude Jekyll's plan for Wall 18 north.

The planting in Wall 18 South starts with an *Artemisia schmidtiana* 'Nana', dark pink dianthus and double arabis. Rock pinks (Miss Jekyll's name for dianthus on these plans) white and pale yellow snaps (her name for snapdragons) continue the planting up to the steps that divide this wall from Wall 18 North. There the planting starts with alyssum, yellow snaps and double arabis. I use *Arabis caucasica*. These plants are followed by *Nepeta mussinii* which needs regular controlling,

without which it would happily fill the entire wall. Verbascum grow near the base of the wall but are not happy in this cramped position. Then white snaps lead through *Arenaria montana* and *Tunica saxifraga* to where the taller part of the wall is mortar-filled. At the base of these walls *Iris stylosa* and plumbago [*Ceratostigma plumbaginoides*] form a footing. Again I have used the words Miss Jekyll wrote on the plans and have added botanical names in parentheses.

Above left: Ceratostigma plumbaginoides. This is an attractive compact species that provides good foliage and beautiful bright blue flowers at the end of summer.

Above centre: Flower heads of Artemisia schmidtiana 'Nana'.

Right: Artemisia schmidtiana 'Nana' in wall 18 south. These are from the great plant family known as 'Wormwoods'. The whole family is noted for its extreme bitterness which accounts for the ancient proverb 'As bitter as wormwood'.

Below left: Arabis caucasica flower.

Below centre: Nepeta mussinii.

THE TENNIS AND BOWLING LAWN WALL

From the Rose Arbour beyond the tennis lawn we have one of my favourite views of house and garden. From this aspect one can appreciate Miss Jekyll's skills in designing a garden that blends with both architecture and nature.

The tennis and bowling lawns are simply marked on plans as two grass areas. This gentle expanse of green runs from the foot of the main walls towards the tennis arbour and provides a good perspective for the views back to the house and its surrounding garden. Miss Jekyll designed a small, 30cm high, drystone wall to absorb the slight slope between the tennis and bowling lawns. There are three very shallow steps in the centre that are typical of her eye for proportion. She believed that an ideal step had a three inch rise and fifteen inch tread (8cm and 38cm) which is not only visually pleasing but practical for walking with wheelbarrows.

The small wall makes a very important break in the wide green grass mass and I love it. But on her plans she wrote 'Thrown out while doing the rest of the work in 1909.'

Left: Bowls on the Bowling Lawn.

Opposite: Walls 18 south and north from the Bowling Lawn in June.

Disregarding the 'thrown out' instruction we built the wall in 1995. It serves as an example of how awkward a client can be. If he does not wish to carry out plans to the full he does not – but I dare say he still declares he has a Gertrude Jekyll garden and there is not much the designer can, or can be inclined to do, to refute that. The plants in this wall are *Veronica buxifolia [Hebe buxifolia], Arenaria montana,* dwarf lavender, rock pinks, *Iberis sempervirens,* santolina, *Campanula carpatica* and an unusual flower, stobaea. Only my informed gardening friends knew that this plant is now known as berkheya and that the cultivar I should use is *Berkheya purpurea.* It has a strange charm. Very prickly stems hold aggressively spiky leaves and the flower is a pale purple, daisy shape, about 8cm across.

The footing at the base of the small wall holds *Iris stylosa,* plumbago [*Ceratostigma plumbaginoides*] and lavender.

Above left: Iberis sempervirens a very easy and attractive edging plant.

Below left: Veronica buxifolia [Hebe buxifolia].

Below right: Lavandula angustifolia 'Munstead', named after Miss Jekyll's own garden at Munstead Wood.

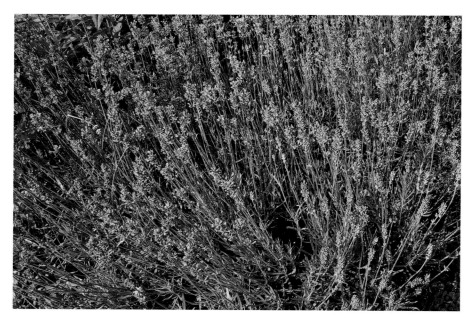

Stobaea [Berkheya purpurea]. A bit of a show-stopper, like a pantomine dame, not good-looking but colourful and interesting.

Shallow steps in the Bowling Lawn wall showing the practical proportions that Miss Jekyll advocated.

Below: Gertrude Jekyll's plan for the Bowling Lawn wall.

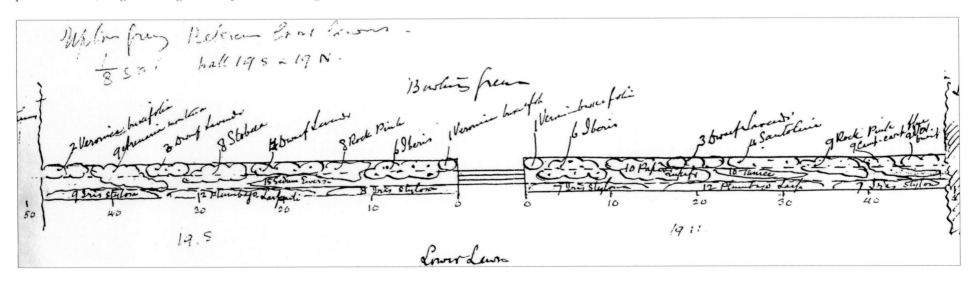

CHAPTER FOUR

The Main Herbaceous Borders

'For planting the ground is painting the landscape with living things.'

Every year visitors express amazement that a garden designed almost one hundred years ago can rank alongside today's finest gardens. They admire the strong simplicity of Miss Jekyll's design, her acceptance and use of new plant material from around the world, and her artistic use of drifts of colour to paint her landscapes. She wrote that art must change, and that people who were unwilling to accept those changes were like those who enjoyed the music of Bach but were unable to accept the beauty of modern instruments and music. She had a way of trusting nature and of always being aware that it was often man's interference with nature that led to disappointing results. She wrote that plants were often 'passive agents in their own misuse.'

Right: Across to Border 2 along the yew hedge in June.

Opposite: Closer over Border 2 in August. The main herbaceous borders are taking over from the plants in the Rose Garden. The colours here will be predominantly strong hot oranges, reds and golds.

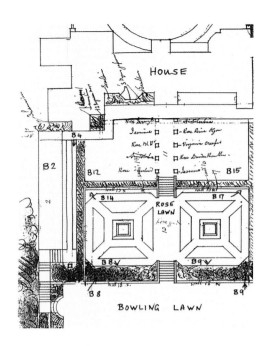

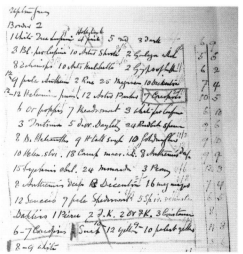

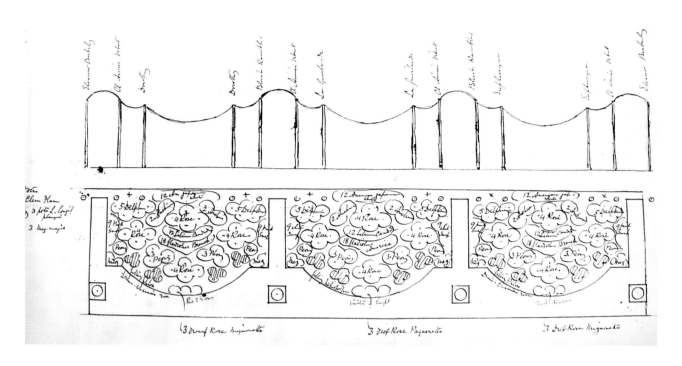

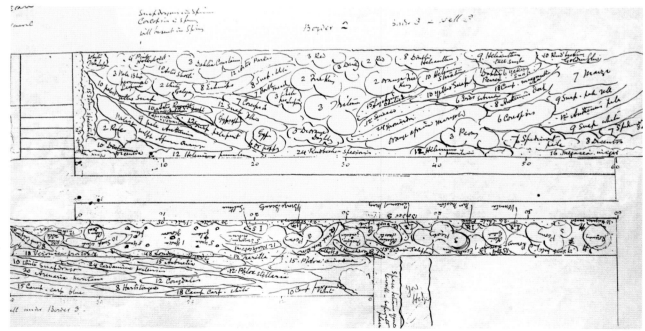

Above: Gertrude Jekyll's plan showing position of Border 2.

Munstead Wood nursery's plant list for Border 2.

Above right: Gertrude Jekyll's plan for mystery Border 1.

Right: Gertrude Jekyll's plan for Border 2 (which I use).

BORDER 2
'Art should work to conceal its art.'
'L'art des sacrifices.'

Although Miss Jekyll drew plans for a Border 1, I have always referred to it as the 'mystery border.' It seems it is an alternative to Border 5 because early photographs show it in situ. It is rather too elaborate and does not balance with its mirror border so I am illustrating her plan and including three early photographs that belonged to Charles Holme's family. They are all dated about 1910-1915. The first is taken from the north-east end of the border, the following two (all poor quality) show the border in the distance with only the rising hoops that supported roses evident. Future gardeners can judge for themselves whether it is worth reinstating, or even inserting somewhere in the garden that is outside the area of Miss Jekyll's plans. On its own it seems quite a beautiful border, but in situ it looks out of place and quite out of character.

I can find no plant lists that show plants provided for Border 1 amongst Miss Jekyll's nursery catalogues for Upton Grey. That surprises me. Had it been a later addition I wonder why she would have named it Border 1. Surely that number would be given to the first border she designed? Another conundrum is that evidently Charles Holme, (or Mr Best), planted it where Border 5 now lies. The fact that the plan was used is evident and the typed list that the University of Berkeley holds with the Manor House plans starts with Item 1 and it does list plants on that plan. Despite this the Munstead Wood's nursery lists show that no plants were provided for that border.

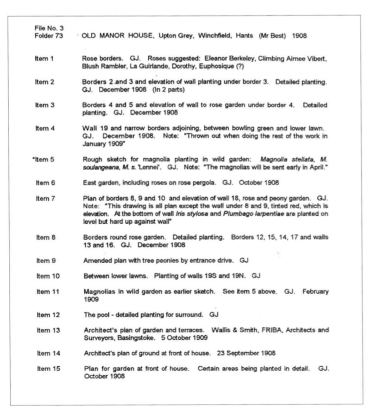

File No. 3
Folder 73 · OLD MANOR HOUSE, Upton Grey, Winchfield, Hants (Mr Best) 1908

Item 1	Rose borders. GJ. Roses suggested: Eleanor Berkeley, Climbing Aimee Vibert, Blush Rambler, La Guirlande, Dorothy, Euphosique (?)
Item 2	Borders 2 and 3 and elevation of wall planting under border 3. Detailed planting. GJ. December 1908 (In 2 parts)
Item 3	Borders 4 and 5 and elevation of wall to rose garden under border 4. Detailed planting. GJ. December 1908
Item 4	Wall 19 and narrow borders adjoining, between bowling green and lower lawn. GJ. December 1908. Note: "Thrown out when doing the rest of the work in January 1909"
*Item 5	Rough sketch for magnolia planting in wild garden: *Magnolia stellata, M. soulangeana, M. s. 'Lennei'*. GJ. Note: "The magnolias will be sent early in April."
Item 6	East garden, including roses on rose pergola. GJ. October 1908
Item 7	Plan of borders 8, 9 and 10 and elevation of wall 18, rose and peony garden. GJ. Note: "This drawing is all plan except the wall under 8 and 9, tinted red, which is elevation. At the bottom of wall *Iris stylosa* and *Plumbago larpentiae* are planted on level but hard up against wall"
Item 8	Borders round rose garden. Detailed planting. Borders 12, 15, 14, 17 and walls 13 and 16. GJ. December 1908
Item 9	Amended plan with tree peonies by entrance drive. GJ
Item 10	Between lower lawns. Planting of walls 19S and 19N. GJ
Item 11	Magnolias in wild garden as earlier sketch. See item 5 above. GJ. February 1909
Item 12	The pool - detailed planting for surround. GJ
Item 13	Architect's plan of garden and terraces. Wallis & Smith, FRIBA, Architects and Surveyors, Basingstoke. 5 October 1909
Item 14	Architect's plan of ground at front of house. 23 September 1908
Item 15	Plan for garden at front of house. Certain areas being planted in detail. GJ. October 1908

Far left: Berkeley University's 'List of Folders' for the garden which mentions roses for Border 1 but no other plants.

Left: A 1916 photograph of Border 1, located where Border 5 now sits.

Photographs of the garden taken after 1920 show no sign of it at all. Perhaps that is why, in 1984, we found, not yew hedging behind Border 5, but a *Cupressocyparis* x *leylandii,* although the rest of the hedging that surrounded the Formal garden was, where it had survived, yew.

One explanation is that the plans, which included the plan for Border 5, remained here until the Savill family, or later occupants, took over. Did they return to Miss Jekyll's simpler shaped border, if not to her planting?

She gave other alternative plantings for this garden. I chose to follow the simplest, but future gardeners could restore to the other plantings as the plans are in safe keeping at the University of Berkeley in California.

On the other side of the Rose Garden, the planting in Border 2, which is one of the two main herbaceous borders, is typical of Miss Jekyll's use of colour, texture and shape in her formal designs.

She described the principles of this planting in *Colour in the Flower Garden,* published in 1908 under that title and reprinted as *Colour Schemes for the Flower Garden* in 1914. This border, and its mirror Border 5, take over the flowering season from the Rose Garden, and their colourful displays continue until the start of winter.

In her introduction to that book Miss Jekyll wrote:

'To plant and maintain a flower border with good scheme for colour, is by no means the easy thing that is commonly supposed. I believe that the only way in which it can be made successful is to devote certain borders to certain times of year; each border or garden region to be bright for from one to three months.'

I take great comfort in that!

Border 2 and its mirror Border 5 are 60 feet [18.3m] long and 10 feet [3.5m] deep. This is not quite long enough to display her planting properly. Her main borders at Munstead Wood (177 feet [54m] by 12 feet [3.6m]) and in other large gardens were often far longer, allowing colours to run into each other gently and for a fine perspective as one looks along the border. At Upton Grey the land slopes too steeply and had to be banked up to form a flat level. It would have been very expensive and impractical to extend that into a longer border.

In a relatively large garden there is space for areas to take their turn in performing, and then to give way to an alternative border in a different season. This technique cannot be applied successfully in a small garden.

Miss Jekyll designed several small town gardens and there her art was intelligently altered. Seasonal plantings gave way to more use of evergreen shrubs, planted pots, structure, and often one beautiful tree whose bark and shape performed well through the seasons. She advised that a small garden should focus on

'items that arrest, sustain interest. If too simply treated a small garden soon exhausts our curiosity.'

Where our plans show a name that I cannot trace in today's encyclopaedias, I refer to J. Weathers' *Practical Guide to Garden Plants,* published by Longmans Green and Co. in 1901. It has been an invaluable reference book for work in this garden. I have three copies, none expensive, so I assume it was printed in large numbers and evidently popular in its day.

In most of her gardens Miss Jekyll used bergenia to edge borders; a plant she knew as megasea, and she included *Megasea major* on these plans. The only reference to *M. major* is in the Munstead Wood plant catalogue where it is described as *'Megasea cordifolia purpurea major.'* *M. cordifolia* was a popular species at that time so I used *Bergenia cordifolia* here. I admire the plant for its fine, strong, heart-shaped leaves. The evergreen leaves are sometimes deep pink-red at the

Opposite: These photographs from 1918 are interesting since they show the looped roses (to the right of the picture) that are part of Border 1 plan.

Opposite below: Another view of Border 1 showing trained over-iron hoops to the right of the picture, in front of the cottage roof.

Left: Across to Border 2 in August showing how the colours run in drifts with cooler colours at either end.

Below: Bergenia cordifolia leaf. This is one of Miss Jekyll's favourite edging plants in any soil.

edge and that colour spreads towards the leaf centre at the end of summer. The pale pink flowers are pretty but of less importance. They seem to flower too early here and are often frizzled back to black panicles by spring frosts.

In the centre of the border the front edges are planted with *Helenium pumilum* which is an autumnal variety. This raises the height of the edges towards the centre of the bed in mid and late summer, and they fill that space with a blaze of yellow. Gertrude Jekyll described how she liked colours to run in drifts from one end of the border to the other, starting with the cool colours, white, blue and pink, moving through to hotter colours, yellow, orange and brilliant red.

Above: Helenium pumilum flower.

Right: Helenium pumilum group in Border 2, a favourite flower for the bees.

From the 'hot' centre the colours run in reverse to cool again at the far end. It is like a crescendo in music and the effect is quite beautiful in its season. The composer Felix Mendelssohn was a friend of the Jekyll family and a frequent visitor to their first house in Grafton Street, London. Gertrude, too, loved music and used analogies with music when describing the art of gardening.

This border faces north-east so includes shade-tolerant plants. Border 5 opposite, although similar in colour and shape, faces south-west and holds more sun-loving plants. A yew hedge surrounds the entire planned Formal Garden and makes a good framework that both protects and displays the planting.

At the back of Border 2 grow the taller herbaceous plants. The role of the main herbaceous borders is to take over from the Rose Garden area which is in flower from late spring to early summer. Borders 2 and 5 continue the season and flower during late summer, autumn and on until the first frosts.

Rudbeckia laciniata 'Golden Glow' stands at the back of the border beside tall single *Helianthus x laetiflorus* 'Miss Mellish', and a double helianthus which is *H. x multiflorus*. About half of the rudbeckia and helianthus are given the 'Chelsea Chop' in late May and a few more are cut back later in June. This reduction of height prolongs the flowering season but more importantly it controls the scale of heights at the back of borders at the end of summer.

In the centre back of the border grow three groups of hollyhocks [*Alcea rosea*] which are also known as althaea from the Greek 'althaia' meaning a healer. They are red and dark red, and they mark the climax of hot colours. They are followed by Aster 'Parker', Dahlia 'Constantine' and finally white tree lupin which run with plants whose colours become cooler towards the end at the back of the border.

Above left: Rudbeckia laciniata 'Golden Glow'. Stems of the helianthus and rudbekia can be bent over flowers that have died back. They will hide a gap and flower along the bent stem. Miss Jekyll advised this use of some tall herbaceous plants in 'Wood and Garden'.

Above centre: Helianthus x laetiflorus 'Miss Mellish'. This healianthus is so invasive that we grow them in sunken pots in the borders.

Above right: Helianthus x multiflorus 'Loddon Gold'. This helianthus is far more manageable.

Left: Hollyhock [Althaea], very English, very 'cottage garden' and very important in late summer.

In total Miss Jekyll used four dahlias at Upton Grey. They are D. 'Fire King', D. 'Orange Fire King', D. 'Percia' and D. 'Constantine.' She knew the value of the sometimes unfashionable dahlia and she wrote with humour of this valuable plant in chapter ten, *September*, of her first book *Wood and Garden*, published by Longmans, Green and Company, in 1899.

'Dahlias are now at their full growth. To make a choice for one's own garden, one must see the whole plant growing. As with many another kind of flower, nothing is more misleading than the evidence of the show-table, for many that there look the best, and are indeed lovely in form and colour as individual blooms, come from plants that are of no garden value. For however charming in humanity is the virtue modesty, and however becoming is the unobtrusive bearing that gives evidence of its possession, it is quite misplaced in a Dahlia. Here it becomes a vice, for the Dahlia's first duty in life is to flaunt and to swagger and to carry gorgeous blooms well above its leaves, and on no account to hang its head.'

She continued with good advice on the staking of these tall plants – another lesson I took far too long to learn.

'Careful and strong staking they must always have, not forgetting one central stake to secure the main growth at first......Its height out of the ground should be about eighteen inches less than the expected stature of the plant. As the Dahlia grows, there should be at least three outer stakes at such distance from the middle as may suit the bulk and habit of the plant; and it is a good plan to have wooden hoops to tie to these, so as to form a girdle round the whole plant and for tying out the outer branches.'

Miss Jekyll also used dahlias to hide a place where an earlier-flowering plant has 'turned brown'. She explained that around such a space:

'Dahlias have been planted, that will be gradually trained down over the space of the departed Sea-Holly; and other Dahlias are used in the same way to mask various weak places.'

Below left: Dahlias and hollyhocks in border 2.

Below right: My modern dahlia, a substitute for Miss Jekyll's 'Orange Fire King', a modern hybrid.

She used this trick with other flowers. Writing of the sunflower she suggested that it is 'of great value to train down, when it throws up a short flowering stem from each joint, and becomes a spreading sheet of bloom'. It is quite evident from the many photographs of Miss Jekyll's borders that her staking is both effective and completely invisible when plants are fully grown. In the area near the dahlias Miss Jekyll plans show Asters 'Shortii', 'Rycroft', 'Parker' and *Aster acris [sedifolious]*. I am told that, like some of the cultivars of *Iris germanica*, asters and dahlias suffered a disease in the early twentieth century and that several are now lost. I can find none of the above except *Aster acris* so I have used four old varieties which I bought from Rosie Hardy of Hardy Plants, in Whitchurch, Hampshire; they are *Aster frikartii, Aster novae-angliae* 'Barr's Blue', 'Treasure' and 'Mrs T. Wright.' These asters, like other tough survivors from the past, need strict control as their roots run rapidly among their less aggressive neighbours.

Perhaps that is another reason why many of the old aster cultivars are lost; they may ask too much work of today's gardeners. In *Wood and Garden* Miss Jekyll wrote

'The Michaelmas Daisies are re-planted every year as soon as their bloom is over, the ground having been newly dug and manured. The old roots, which will have increased about four-fold, are pulled or chopped to pieces, nice bits with about five crowns being chosen for re-planting.'

I don't do it that often – but probably should.

Above left: a close-up view of Aster x frikartii 'Monch'.

Above right: Aster x frinkartii 'Monch'.

Left: Aster acris [A. sedifolius]. All these asters flower well in shady areas.

Above: the magnificent leaves of Zea mays 'variegata'.

Right: Zea mays 'variegata' in Border 2. This is a wonderful autumnal annual but it does need a sunny position for its dark maroon cobs to ripen and set seed for the following year.

The central run of planting in this border is slightly lower but by no means uniform in height. It starts with 'Maize' on her plans. I was assured by experienced gardeners that Miss Jekyll used the variegated *Zea mays var 'Japonica'*, a lovely annual plant. Initially it was hard to find a source but after a few years an American friend gave me seeds. This *Zea mays* does not always ripen in an English summer, but we grow extra plants in the sunniest part of the kitchen garden and keep the dark maroon cobs from year to year as a safety back-up. In late summer the green–yellow–purple veined leaves stand tall and magnificent towards the back of the borders. Obviously it has to be grown annually. It is started in pots in the greenhouse. We heat the Bolton and Paul greenhouse economically with a simple Calor gas heater which, for most of the time, is only switched on at night. On one bench we run heated electric cables to aid seed germination. We do not use any heat until 14th February and we switch off all heat in mid May.

At Upton Grey, as in most of her gardens, Miss Jekyll used annuals and they prove extremely useful, not only in

Left: Campanula latifolia var macrantha (flower close).

Above: Campanula latifolia var macrantha (group). There are four different campanula species in this garden. It is a genus of great variety.

providing colour throughout the summer, but also in expanding into areas where plants have failed or flower later in the year. She recommended 'fillings snaps' [antirrhinum] in places, and I do this with license. By sowing successively (generally a few seeds every three weeks) we have maize, marigolds, snapdragons and other annuals ready to plant out from May until August. Yellow snaps grow beside the maize and behind *Campanula macrantha* [*C. latifolia*].

Today's snapdragons tend to be too small. In *Wood and Garden* Miss Jekyll wrote about *'the podgy little dwarf Snapdragons,'* and she confessed a liking for the

'ungraceful little dumpy things because they have come in some tender colourings of pale yellow and pale pink that give them an absurd prettiness.'

I have found that most modern yellow snapdragons have a rather harsh colour, so I go to some lengths to select the paler ones for propagation. I keep seeds of the older varieties which can grow to a height of over 60 centimetres.

Some of Miss Jekyll's favourite annuals. Above left to right:What Miss Jekyll humorously described as 'Podgy Snaps'; Nigella damascena (Miss Jekyll's hybrid); Cosmos; Eschscholzia. Below left to right: Papaver rhoeas [Shirley poppy]; Godetia; Callistephus.

In 1916 Miss Jekyll's book *Annuals and Biennials* was published by Country Life, in which she reminded her readers of the value of annuals. Her own *Nigella damascena* 'Miss Jekyll' is illustrated at the front. She described when to sow and how to use some of her favourites, and I am often happily surprised by the reaction of visitors here to rather forgotten old favourites like eschscholzia, *Papaver nudicaule* and *P. rhoeas,* clarkia, cosmos and godetia. These and other plants that Miss Jekyll used in some of her gardens, but not at Upton Grey, I plant in the kitchen garden to provide a riot of colour in mid and late summer. It is a pretty riot but it is not art, because flowers in the kitchen garden are not arranged to a plan. It is simply a holding nursery for plants that may need replacing and, in a few instances, for plants that I wish to get to know. Probably Miss Jekyll had visited too many gardens planted like this – at random. She certainly had a great many plant collectors among her friends and evidently not all were artists in the garden. She wrote:

'A garden made by a collector is very rarely beautiful. A quantity of plants does not make a garden it only makes a collection.'

The rest of the border comprises, in order of planting, *Tradescantia virginiana* deep and pale blue, which she called Spiderwort, *Dicentra spectabilis*, *Coreopsis grandiflora*, *Iris sibirica*, more dahlias, *Lychnis chalcedonica* and *Senecio* [*Cineraria maritima*].

Above left: Dicentra spectabilis.
Above right: Coreopsis grandiflora.
Below left: Tradescantia virginiana.
Below centre: Cineraria maritima [Senecio cineraria].
Below right: Lychnis chalcedonica. This provides a strong bright red at the centre of the main borders and it is virtually trouble free.

Also included in this border are *Monarda didyma, Rudbeckia speciosa, Anthemis tinctoria, Anthemis sancti-johannis* and African marigolds [Tagetes]. Here again annuals prove very useful fillers in the main herbaceous borders. Drifts of African marigolds both yellow and orange make a useful contribution in late summer. By keeping seeds from our African marigolds we grow rather simple, almost single flowers. It seems that the hybrids try to revert to older cultivars with time.

Above: Flower-head of the Monarda didyma.

Right: Monarda didyma group. This simple herbaceous plant, commonly known as bergamot, gives important colour and foliage to a north-facing border at the end of summer and well into autumn.

Above left: African marigold [Tagetes erecta].

Above right: African marigold [Tagetes erecta]. My very single flower which, I suppose, is a result of taking seeds from a different generation of the same plants for several years and 'in-breeding'.

Far left: Anthemis sancti-johannis.

Left: Anthemis tinctoria.

Above left: Gypsophila paniculata is a plant that Miss Jekyll often used beside a plant that flowers and dies early in the year because this fills the space delicately.

Above centre: Kniphofia uvaria.

Above right: Daylily [Hemerocallis fulva 'Kwanso Flore Plena']. This was one of only three plants that I found had survived the century in its original position in the Formal Garden.

Other plants in this area are peonies, tritoma [*Kniphofia uvaria*], Orange Daylilies [*Hemerocallis fulva 'Kwanso Flore Plena'*] and *Gypsophila paniculata*. Miss Jekyll often planted gypsophila beside a flower that was to bloom early and die back. In *Wood and Garden* she wrote, '*Where flowers are over by mid-summer, plant Gypsophila paniculata between and behind …. and by July there is a delicate cloud of bloom instead of large bare patches.*' Here it grows beside the May-flowering Oriental poppy. I use the perennial *Gypsophila paniculata*.

I am annually amused, or irritated, according to the time of day, to find that the Oriental poppy grows so robustly that neighbouring gypsophila is virtually smothered in its infancy.

This is another gardening trick that demands a little more effort in practice. Set-backs discovered early in the day can be a stimulating challenge. Setbacks that occur towards evening when energy levels are low can be exasperating. Those plants are followed by white galega and pale blue perennial lupins (probably the lost *Lupinus polyphyllus* 'Munstead Blue'). I find lupins do not like our regularly composted and manured beds. The soil is probably too rich for them. Lately I have been using Chiltern seeds of *Lupinus polyphyllus* 'The Gardener' which is a bi-colour and, strictly speaking, too late an introduction for this garden. Although they are perennials, lupins are relatively short-lived and I am hoping to find suitable replacements.

The border continues with *Echinops ritro, Filipendula ulmaria, Spiraea venusta* [*Filipendula rubra 'Venusta'*], more dahlias and the three previously mentioned asters.

The taller plants are supported by stakes and sheep wire. Smaller plants grow with the support of wooden poles made from coppiced trees in the nuttery.

Two China Roses grow at the far end of the border and I have chosen 'Old Blush China' because it grows healthily and beautifully on our chalky soil.

Left: Spirea venusta [Filipendula venusta]. As long as the border does not become too dry, both the spirea and the day lilies flower wonderfully mid-summer.

Above centre: Meadowsweet [Filipendula ulmaria]. This almost wild plant does need plenty of water, particularly on our well-drained soil.

Above right: Echinops ritro.

Below centre: Lupinus polyphyllus.

Below right: Echinops ritro flower-head.

BORDER 3
'A constant Hymn of Praise' Wood and Garden

Border 3 runs parallel to Border 2 and continues around and beyond the steps that end it. The curved end tops the tall stone wall which, because of its height, was evidently built into cement backing.

At the edge of this plan Gertrude Jekyll has written 'Other spaces marked '7' in general plan, plant with your laurustinus.' She has written 'plant with your own....' in other places on our plans. Evidently some clients took favourite plants with them when they moved house and perhaps they simply moved surplus stock from place to place in their new garden.

Miss Jekyll developed a successful plant nursery in her own property at Munstead Wood. Godalming Museum in Surrey now holds her hand-written Plant Books. These list the plants she sold and the prices she charged. Miss Jekyll was proud of the competitive rates she offered her clients. The plant lists are also evidence of the enormous amount of work she undertook, because the selection and quantity of plants she could provide is most impressive. For example in 1911 she provided some 600 plants for the artist and critic Roger Fry at Durbins in Guildford. Transporting that number of plants must have proved quite a challenge. Trains were usually her preferred form of transport, but she was still responsible for careful packing and delivery to her local station. A great many plants on the Upton Grey plans were originally supplied from the Munstead Wood nursery, as is evident from the photographs of her plant lists.

Above left: Border 3 in May. The shape of the planting is good but very little has started to flower.

Left: Border 3 in July.

Opposite: Border 3 in June.

The curved area of Border 3 is planted with shrubs and tall plants to form a small alcove. Here, judging by old photographs, a stone bench has been seated for years. One of the plants that fills this rounded area is Rosa 'Blush Gallica', now known as 'Blush Damask'. This is a pretty, double, pink and sweet-smelling rose which at the start of its life here was one of my favourites. But within a decade 'Blush Damask' ran almost out of control in height and width. Its roots scramble for yards through stones and paving.

Perhaps this is Miss Jekyll's unruly area because the other roses, which she calls Scotch Briar *[Rosa pimpinellifolia]*, also fill the space above the high wall and they too make root-runs everywhere. In front of those is Verbascum. I use *Verbascum lychnitis* because it is an old variety that forms a rather elegant, tall, green-grey steeple late summer when much else is over. But I am told that Miss Jekyll may have used *V. olympicu*m or *V. phlomoides* which she described as 'the two best garden Mulliens.'

Three 'Old Blush China' roses, struggle through the tight planting on one side of the six laurustinus bushes and at their feet grow filler plants (although hardly needed) of 24 white

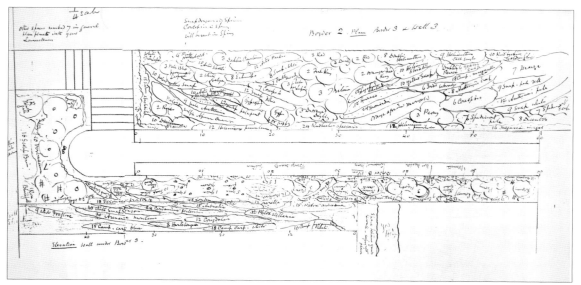

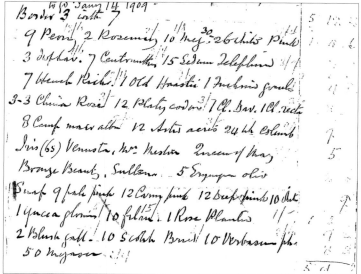

columbines. Laurustinus [*Viburnum tinus*], which is still a popular hedging plant, encloses the area within the briar. I believe that Miss Jekyll slightly over-planted on plans in order to give her gardens early impact. Obviously the filler plants would have become unnecessary, or would have been reduced, with time. Most garden designers work like this.

In 2003 the, generally strong, *Viburnum tinus* and the vigorous *Rosa pimpinellifolia* started to die in places. By 2006 several plants had died completely so I sent plants with roots to the R.H.S. at Wisley and asked for advice. They were unable to identify the cause. By 2008 nearly all plants in that area had died and so had all my 'replacement' plants. I have been told that neither Honey Fungus nor Fire Blight were the cause of the sickness and that it is probably a Phytopthora. I hope the worst is over, but while the few new plants that have been introduced are struggling, the border looks lopsided and unattractive. I call that area 'The Morgue'.

Bergenia grows at the feet of the *Viburnum tinus* and they run on until they meet the edging of pinks where the border narrows. The white columbine that I use is *Aquilegia vulgaris* 'Munstead White' [*A. vulgaris 'Nivea'*] the cultivar

that Miss Jekyll introduced in 1884. It is said not to cross with other colours. I find it does produce a few very pale coloured seedlings if grown near deep aquilegia but the white are strong and easy to maintain.

From the rounded end of Border 3 the plants run as follows towards the house: *Campanula latifolia, Aster acris, Clematis recta, Veronica prostrata, Clematis heracleifolia* var. *davidiana*, antirrhinum sp., *Yucca filamentosa* and *Yucca gloriosa*, London pride [*Saxifraga umbrosa*], *Eryngium oliverianum, Platycodon* var. *mariesii, Tiarella cordifolia, Heuchera richardsonii, Phlox amoena*, peonies and *Sisyrinchium striatum*. Where this border meets the grass on the top terrace the taller shrubs are introduced because the view beyond, over the rose garden, is no longer needed. These plants are *Fuchsia magellanica* var. *gracilis, Olearia* x *haastii* and *Olearia phlogopappa, Centranthus ruber* [valerian], lavender, rosemary and bergenia. All those plants are readily available today. Some grow better than others here and I have to be vigilant in ensuring that weaker plants are not smothered by their neighbours. A back-up supply of nearly every one is kept safely in the kitchen garden in case of disaster.

The border finishes with three of the China rose, Rosa 'Duke of York', and dotted along the border edge are five

bearded iris. Miss Jekyll did not specify which China roses to use so I have, again, chosen roses that were available before 1908.

To return to the south end of the border; the two shrub clematis, *C. recta* and *C. heracleifolia*, have to be controlled yearly and divided every few years. *Yucca filamentosa* grows statuesquely in this bed so that, seen from below in the rose garden, it is magnificent against a blue sky when in flower (and in good weather!). But *Yucca gloriosa*, although it grows well in several other gardens near here, has died back so often that I have allowed *Y. filamentosa* to fill the space. Future gardeners will refer to the plans again and may be more successful.

Eryngium oliverianum is quite my favourite eryngium. It has strong blue heads which are a beautiful sight late summer when so much else is going over. It is worth searching for. It is not one of the commoner eryngiums but can be found in some of Britain's plant nurseries and it is listed in *The Plant Finder*, which is compiled by The Royal Horticultural Society. *Eryngium oliverianum* was quite rare when we started restoring the garden. In the September 1998 issue of the American magazine, *Traditional Home*, Elvin McDonald wrote an article entitled 'Sea Holly Aristocrats.' It included the following sentence:

'More recently, on a midsummer pilgrimage to English gardens, my camera's eye was drawn to the exquisite …almost unreal purple-veined vivid blue of E. *oliverianum* at Manor House, Upton Grey. Upton Grey is a 1908 Gertrude Jekyll garden that is alive and well in the hands - nicely calloused - of Rosamund Wallinger.' That proved to me again how valuable our nurseries and our old cottage gardens are – and that the garden's appearance is rather more important than mine!

The fuchsia, like many of the plants in this border, perform well from late summer until well into autumn. The three shrubs that grow beyond it, the two olearias and the rosemary, are evergreen and they add valuable winter structure to the garden. Miss Jekyll described July as a difficult month. She wrote:

(In July) 'there seems to be a time of comparative emptiness between the earlier flowers and those of autumn.'

I would add my own comment that August usually requires more work for less reward.

Above: Eryngium oliverianum flower.
Left: Eryngium oliverianum in Border 3 in late June.

BORDER 4

'She more than any other has made the planting of gardens in English speaking countries one of the Fine Arts'.
Mrs Francis King, founder of the Garden Club of America in 1913. Gertrude Jekyll wrote the preface for Mrs King's *The Well-Considered Garden*. Mrs. King wrote using her married name. (Louisa Yeomans King was her full name).

The design of Border 4 is similar to Border 3 with slight changes in planting that give a similar and balanced effect.

The curved end is planted to match exactly with Border 3. *Viburnum tinus* shelters a stone seat and again low-growing plants fill the centre of the bed, in order not to interrupt the view over the Rose Garden beneath.

At the southern end, white snapdragons (snaps) lead to *Chrysanthemum [Leucanthemum] maximum*, Delphinium Belladonna Group *[Delphinium parryi]*, then on to groups of *Yucca filamentosa*. These are followed by snaps yellow and pink that grow on either side of an eryngium. Then peonies, centranthus and deep pink snaps lead to *Spirea Venusta [Filipendula rubra]*. At this point the border no longer

Borders 4 and 5 in late summer. To keep herbaceous plants upright in the main borders we have supported most with stakes cut from the Nuttery and sheep-fencing wire.

Opposite: Borders 4 and 5 in May. The shape is good but the full summer colours have not yet started.

overlooks the rose garden so the following taller plants and shrubs are introduced, *Fuchsia Riccartonii*, *Olearia* x *haastii*, *Clematis heracleifolia* var *davidiana* and Phlox 'Avalanche'. I could not find that phlox so chose a white *Phlox paniculata* 'White Admiral'. Recently I have been told that Phlox 'Avalanche' is *P. maculata* 'Schneelawine' (German for an avalanche!) so that will be corrected. From there to the end the bed is filled with peonies, *Campanula latifolia*, more snapdragons, *Olearia Gunnii [O. phlogopappa]* and, to balance with Border 3 opposite, the China rose 'Duke of York.' The border is edged with nepeta, pinks, bergenia and *Polygonum brunonis [Persicaria affine]*; here we use the cultivar 'Donald Lowndes'.

Right: Laurustinus [Viburnum tinus]. This is a strong evergreen shrub that Miss Jekyll often used. I believed it was almost indestructable until a phytophthora disease caught it.

Below left: Munstead Wood nursery's plant list for Border 4.

Below right: Gertrude Jekyll's plan for Borders 4 and 5.

Opposite: Borders 4 and 5 in June. Note how yew hedging gives strong outline to the Formal Garden.

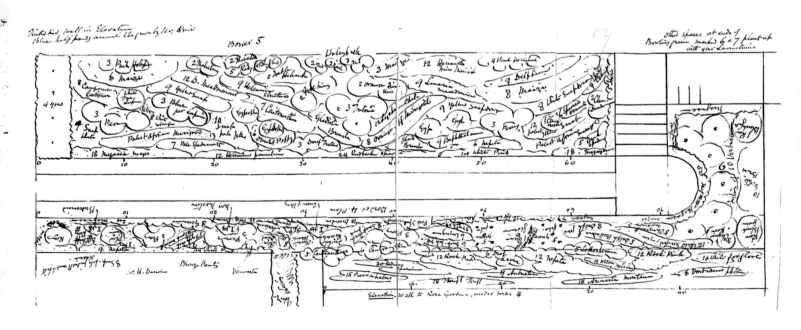

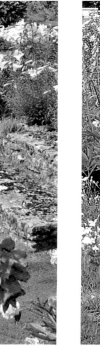

Clockwise: Chrysanthemum maximum [Leucanthemum maximum]; Delphinium Belladonna group; Campanula latifolia, blue and white; Phlox paniculata, group; Phlox paniculata, flower-head; Lithospermum rosmarinifolia.

Miss Jekyll has written '8 geranium' on her plan but does not specify which geranium, so I took a piece from one growing at the pond in 1984 which I was told was an old *Geranium macrorrhizum* and I added a *Geranium cinereum* var *subcaulescens*. *Lithospermum [Lithodora] rosmarinifolia* and *Dicentra spectabilis* finish the edging and, amongst all those plants, six clumps of bearded iris are planted at regular intervals.

Above left: Polygonum affine 'Donald Lowndes'.
Above right: Spirea venusta, group.
Left: Geranium macrorrhizum.
Right: Geranium cinereum flower.

BORDER 5

'If you take any flower you please and look it over and turn it about and smell it and feel it and try to find out all its little secrets, not of flower only but of leaf, bud and stem as well, you will discover many wonderful things. This is how to make friends with plants and very good friends you will find them to the end of our lives.' Children and Gardens

This border is positioned to the north-east side of the Rose Garden and faces south-west. It is backed by the two metre high yew hedge [*Taxus baccata*] which gives shelter and good backdrop to the flowers. For those reasons yew is a hedging that Miss Jekyll used often in her gardens.

In describing this border I am using the names Miss Jekyll wrote on her plans and adding the current name where necessary.

From the back at the northern end of the border the planting starts with pink hollyhocks and variegated maize. They are followed by Thalictrum. (I have chosen to use *Thalictrum aquilegifolium* although Miss Jekyll may have intended *Thalictrum flavum* or *Thalictrum delavayi*). This is a fine tall, strongly-stemmed plant which is headed by a cloud of tiny pale purple flowers that have no petals, but tufts of prominent stamens that perform prettily throughout the summer. It makes a very good border plant and it needs little support. It does tend to set seeds all around itself but those seedlings are easy to control and I will put up with a lot from a beautiful plant that doesn't collapse in wind and rain.

In Border 5 and its mirror Border 2 the planting can become thick and unruly by mid-summer. Miss Jekyll was well aware of the need for control both in thinning and staking. She warned that:

'with lack of attention to thinning, a border becomes untidy and the beauty of the individual groups is lost.'

It took me some time to realise this and to exercise necessary control.

Tall and generally late-flowering plants continue to fill the back of the border. *Rudbeckia laciniata* 'Golden Glow' is followed by double helianthus. I use *Helianthus* x *multiflorus* 'Loddon Gold'. I am not sure of its date of introduction but it is strong, healthy and fits very well in this planting. Deep red hollyhocks follow those, to give height and hot colour to the back of the border and at their feet, to hide unsightly stalks late summer, grow dahlias and Tritoma, [*Kniphofia uvaria* and *Kniphofia* x *praecox*]. Two more groups of strong orange and red dahlias follow those.

The invasive *Helianthus* x *laetiflorus* 'Miss Mellish' is the next plant and beyond that grow paler hollyhocks and blue delphinium making the colours drift out to cool again. Other drifts of plants that run from the northern end of the border are *Campanula lactiflora* which is a great favourite with visitors in middle to late summer, *Centranthus ruber*, white tree lupin and blue perennial

Above: Border 5 in September. The main borders still look fine in September but without their supporting stakes plants would virtually collapse.

Below: Gertrude Jekyll's plan for Border 5.

Opposite: Border 5 in July.

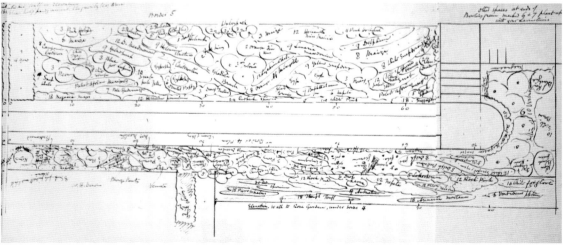

Above: Munstead Wood nursery's plant list for Border 5.

Left: Papaver orientale.

Opposite: Overlooking Borders 4 and 5 to kitchen garden and orchard beyond in June.

lupin, yellow snap (Miss Jekyll never writes antirrhinum or snapdragon on these plans) and double meadowsweet [*Filipendula ulmaria*]. The hot colours, yellow, red and orange follow in *Helenium striatum [Helenium autumnale], Lychnis chalcedonica* which is a wonderful fiery red and has the double blessing of needing little or no support, orange African marigolds, *Gladiolus x brenchleyensis, Buphthalmum salicifolium* and oriental poppies which, as in Border 2, are surrounded by gypsophila. *Gladiolus* x *brenchleyensis* was considered lost to the horticultural world until 2005 when Professor Michael Tooley found it growing on the Isle of Man and reintroduced it to the Royal Horticultural Society who confirmed it correct. I have found that the plants I was given are not strong and are

rarely winter-hardy. Their corms need to be allowed to dry before being taken into the greenhouse for protection each winter, which presumably accounts for their rarity today.

Miss Jekyll advised using *Linaria macedonica* in this border I was unable to find that species so by lucky instinct I chose to use *Linaria dalmatica*. In my bible, *The New Royal Horticultural Society's Dictionary of Gardening* (1992 edition), I discovered that they are one and the same. This luck also applied to my decision to plant the rose Rosa 'Blush Damask' in place of Rosa 'Blush Gallica'. Those names, also, had interchanged. Perhaps a bit of Miss Jekyll's spirit was getting through to me.

This edition of *The New RHS Dictionary of Gardening* has been invaluable. I bought it soon after publication. It has been quite an extravagant investment for the owner of a small garden. I bought it in a fit of pique with my husband for some minor disagreement and I paid for it on his account. I have never regretted the purchase but am not proud of the fit of pique! He is too generous to complain.

Towards the end of the border, colours run out to cooler yellow, blue and white through pale yellow African marigolds, peonies, *Clematis recta*, *Spiraea Venusta* [*Filipendula rubra 'Venusta'*], *Clematis heracleifolia* var. *davidiana*, pale spiderwort [*tradescantia*], white columbines [*aquilegia*] and finally *Iberis sempervirens*.

The plants that edge this border are similar to those in Border 2. Bergenia, which fills each end, drifts into *Helenium pumilum*, *Rudbeckia speciosa*, now known as *Rudbekia fulgida* var. *speciosa*, and then white pinks [dianthus].

I give visitors to the garden a printed guide which lists every plant and the border in which it grows. But gardeners may still be perplexed by the sea of plants in a given area. I tried using labels but found they disappear in high summer and the temptation to people to struggle into the border to find a lost label can be irresistible. In Chapter Ten of *Home and Garden*, Gertrude

Above left: Althea [hollyhocks] and dahlias in Border 5.
Below left: Thalictrum aquilegifolium, a simple, trouble-free self-supporting plant.
Below right: Bupthalmum salicifolium.

Jekyll recommends *'driving the ugly thing* [the label] *into the earth, leaving only just enough above ground to lay hold of.'* It is good advice for the gardener who needs to remember the names of plants – but not for one who opens their garden to visitors.

Miss Jekyll wrote that:

> *'The thing that matters is that in its season a border shall be kept full and beautiful and by what means does not the least matter.'* She acknowledged that *'all gardening is the reward of well directed and strongly sustained effort.'*

She also made the important point that *'all gardening requires constant change'* because *'There is change and growth in all art.'* She wanted her readers to keep an open mind on all aspects of gardening art. She knew that art should not be locked in time and style, and she made the interesting comparison with music when talking of the formal, architectural, gardeners. *'The champions of the formal garden would stop at the music of Bach.'* In other words Bach's music may have been the finest of its time but the introduction of new instruments, like the great range of new plants from around the world, has expanded the art of both music and gardens.

Above right: Gladiolus brenchleyensis.
Below left: Linaria dalmatica.
Below centre: Campanula lactiflora, flower-head.
Below right: Campanula lactiflora, group.

CHAPTER FIVE

The Pergola, the Rose Arbour and Surrounding Garden

'I hold that the best purpose of a garden is to give delight and to give refreshment of mind, to soothe, to refine and to lift up the heart.' Wood and Garden

THE PERGOLA
'Formality but never fussed'

A pergola leads from the house to central steps that descend to the Rose Garden. The ten sturdy wooden posts are 15cm square. They stand just over two metres high and 160cm apart. They are each topped with a brass pipe-holder, bought from a plumbers' merchants, through which hang thick ships' ropes of about 8-10cm diameter. Like most of the Jekyll pergolas that I have seen illustrated in her books, this is a strong, purposeful structure that runs the architecture of the house into the formal garden and which holds its abundant planting securely.

The planting is interesting and surprisingly varied for a limited pergola. On each side every post holds a different climbing plant but the effect, far from being muddled is in fact quite splendid at certain times of the year.

The posts that face west hold first, a pretty, single, climbing rose with pale yellow flowers, Rosa 'Jersey Beauty'. It has strong, shiny dark green leaves and although not an abundant repeat flowerer does produce flowers well on into the late summer. That is followed by Jasmine which, when in flower, fills the area with scent. We have used *Jasminum officinale*; it needs controlling as it is a vigorous grower, but cutting it back each year is a simple job and does it no harm. I have been told that this jasmine is one of the invasive weeds that the British settlers introduced to New Zealand in the nineteenth century

Opposite: The pergola, west side, in June with climbers, from left to right – Rosa 'Jersey Beauty', Jasmine, Rosa 'Blush Rambler', Aristolochia macrophylla, Rosa 'The Garland'.

Below left: The pergola east side with climbers: Jasmine, Rosa 'Dundee Rambler', Parthenocissus quinquefolia, Rosa 'Reine Olga de Würtemburg', Aristolochia macrophylla.

Below right: Overlooking the pergola in late June.

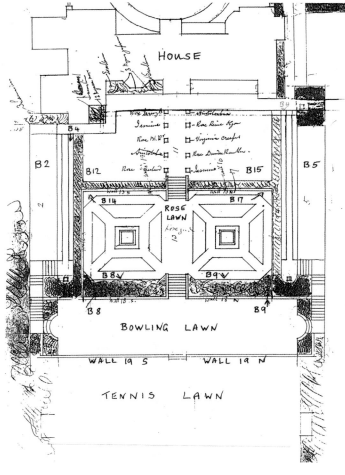

Gertrude Jekyll's plan for the pergola.

Munstead Wood nursery's plant list for the pergola.

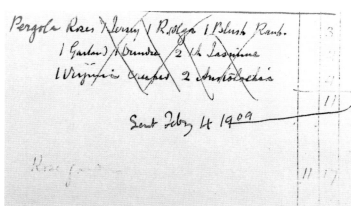

– a warning to me and visitors that taking plants abroad without declaring them to customs can be very dangerous.

One of my favourite rambling roses, Rosa 'Blush Rambler', follows the jasmine. When I bought it from Harkness in 1985 their catalogue described it as 'lost, until found in a cottage garden in Bedfordshire.' From that I learnt the importance of those beloved cottage gardens, whose owners cared for plants whether or not they were fashionable, and which provided Miss Jekyll with so many valuable garden plants.

Aristolochia macrophylla grows up the next post. It is known as 'Dutchman's Pipe' because of the curious shape of its flower. The name derives from the Greek 'aristos', meaning best and 'lochos', concerning birth, because of the believed value of some species in aiding childbirth. Every year visitors search for the small green flower. It is hard to find amongst the large green leaves and I have never seen one pollinated, so I imagine the bees have a problem too. Aristolochia was the most expensive plant in the garden in 1984. With very little money to spare after we had made the almost derelict house habitable I had to buy two plants for £10.00 each. That was an enormous sum compared to the price I paid for the packets of seeds that supplied plants for over half the garden. (In those days a packet of seeds from my favourite source, Chiltern Seeds, cost about 30 pence so I was able to fill the Formal Garden for £20.00 and have money left over to buy small shrubs).

The last pergola post holds one of Gertrude Jekyll's favourite rambling roses, Rosa 'The Garland.' She used it time and again in her gardens and several times in our Wild Garden. It was introduced in 1835 and is an early rambler. It is strong, it tolerates hard pruning when necessary and, although it flowers once only, like most ramblers, it does so with such breathtaking vivacity that it astonishes us every year. In winter months it is covered with small red hips, a fitting reminder of its summer efforts.

The other side of the pergola holds jasmine and aristolochia again, although not opposite the same, and then another favourite Jekyll rose, Rosa 'Dundee Rambler.' That is an unusually pure white rose, the branches of which are easily bent to cover the thick ship's rope that leads from post to post. Virginia Creeper *[Parthenocissus quinquefolia]* grows

Clockwise: Rosa 'Jersey Beauty';
Rosa 'Blush Rambler';
Jasminum officinale;
Aristolochia macrophylla.

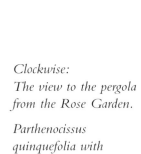

Clockwise:
The view to the pergola
from the Rose Garden.

Parthenocissus
quinquefolia with
autumn-tinted leaves.

Rosa 'The Garland'.

The pergola with
autumn colours in late
September.

Above: Rosa 'Reine Olga de Würtemberg' d.1881.

Right: Rosa 'Dundee Rambler' d. 1850 and dogs.

beside that rose. I was surprised that so vigorous a climber could be used on a relatively small pergola but like its neighbours it tolerates severe pruning and its crimson leaves in late summer and autumn are quite beautiful.

Opposite the jasmine, the last rose on this side is Rosa 'Reine Olga de Würtemberg.' It took me some time to find that rose but, again, I found it with André Êve in France and it justifies its elusiveness annually. Although it has not died it is small, weak and requires a great deal of extra feed and care. I dare say it is missing its country of origin which one supposes is France.

125

THE ROSE ARBOUR

The focal point through the pergola is the arbour on the far side of the tennis lawn. This is made with five chamfered oak posts and covered with roses that were available in Miss Jekyll's time. They are Rosa 'Paul's Himalayan Musk,' a truly spectacular rambling rose when in flower, and Rosa 'Madame Alfred Carrière.' Because this is simply an area marked on her plans with a space from which to watch tennis, Miss Jekyll has not planted it. So I have included Rosa 'American Pillar' in the arbour. I found the rose here. It is happy in its spot so I left it. It was introduced in 1909, so is possibly one year too young for this garden, but its bright pink flowers make a very strong focal point and it clothes the arbour beautifully.

The view from the Rose Garden to the arbour in summer (above) and winter snow (below). Although the Formal Garden lacks something of the Wild Garden's natural, coloured beauty in winter, this scene shows the importance of strong design and structure in a garden. That art was one of Miss Jekyll's legacies to gardens of any size. One focal point should lead to another, either with paths, pergola or edging plants; each plant has a purpose.

Above: The Bolton and Paul greenhouse is the 1898 model.

Above right: The orchard in blossom.

Opposite: The nuttery and bluebells.

AREAS THAT SURROUND
THE PLANNED FORMAL GARDEN

Parts of the garden that surround the Formal Garden are not planned by Miss Jekyll, they are simply places that most Edwardian gardens would include but which, because they are utilitarian or seasonally changing, would not require planning.

The three main areas are the nuttery, which is planted with *Corylus avellana* [the hazelnut tree], the orchard, which has apple, greengage, plum, pear and fig trees, and the kitchen garden. The latter is almost entirely filled with plants from the main herbaceous borders which we hold in custody in case those in the borders weaken. Some are kept as a source of seeds. Divisions of plants or of corms and roots are held in the kitchen garden until they are large enough to move on.

We have an 1898 model Bolton and Paul greenhouse; a fine thing but badly restored with unsuitable wood and it is rotting fast throughout.

A cold frame holds cuttings of roses etc. for root-stock, and if I am given a rare old plant, like the *Gladiolus brenchleyensis*, that too is held safely in an isolated place until I have sufficient offspring to move the plants to their correct positions.

In its season the kitchen garden gives a triumphant display of vibrant colour. A wide grass path leads from one entrance arch to another at the far end, where a few vegetables are permitted. Both arches are festooned with roses that Miss Jekyll used in other gardens. The effect is, as Miss Jekyll wrote of the un–planned, un–artistic garden, *'like paints on an artist's palette'*. It is bright but it is not art, and in winter it is nothing but good brown earth. We used old ships' rope again to hold roses that festoon the edging of that path.

The last part of the garden to be described is Upton Grey's Wild Garden, in which it is apparent how Miss Jekyll used nature 'freely.' This is the part of the garden where she wrote that nature should be left *'untormented'* and where *'the garden should not intrude.'* Rather humorously she also wrote to *'make no parade of conscious effort.'* It is interesting to show examples of both formal and free styles, to compare them, and to ask today's gardeners which they prefer.

Although the Formal Garden does hold some of the

Rose archway to the kitchen garden with Rosa 'Veilchenblau' d.1909 and Rosa 'Felicité Perpétue' d.1827.

Opposite: The centre of the kitchen garden in July. It holds Jekyll herbaceous and annual plants for the main borders.

Towards the old garden shed in the kitchen garden. The central grass path breaks the colourful but random planting, giving some structure and vista to an otherwise rather chaotic area.

The far end of the kitchen garden with 'cloud' edging of rosemary, Santolina and box.

Above: The ships' rope that edges the kitchen garden with climbing roses to form the 'Rope Walk'. The roses on the rope are Mme. Caroline Testout.

Opposite: The far end of the kitchen garden through rose arches to the orchard.

aromatic plants, for instance rosemary and lavender, that Miss Jekyll so admired when on her Mediterranean travels, it is in the Wild Garden that I find a true Mediterranean mood on a warm summer evening. Where *Cistus laurifolius* are grouped beside the winding grass paths they fill the mid-summer air with the rich scents of their leaves and stems. In the following chapter Professor Michael Tooley writes of Miss Jekyll's travels and plant discoveries around the Mediterranean.

CHAPTER SIX

by Professor Michael Tooley

Miss Gertrude Jekyll's Mediterranean travels and plant discoveries, and their use at Upton Grey

Francis Jekyll noted in his memoir of Aunt 'Bumps' that

'there is no doubt that her lifelong partiality for evergreen and aromatic plants – the myrtles, cistuses, salvias, and phlomises with which she surrounded her houses and those of her friends – can be traced directly to the raptures of her first acquaintance with the flora of the Mediterranean sea-board.'
(*Gertrude Jekyll, A Memoir,* Jonathan Cape, 1934).

Opposite: Kniphofia uvaria in the Wild Garden.

Plants originating in the Mediterranean area make a significant contribution to Gertrude Jekyll's plans for the garden of The Manor House as they did for her own home, Munstead Wood, and for many of the four hundred gardens that she designed between 1868 and 1932.

Miss Jekyll is well known for the plants she collected from cottage gardens and the wild in Britain and elsewhere, testing them for their hardiness and as garden-worthy plants. With the exception of rosemary, lavender and some irids, she is perhaps not immediately associated with the rich Mediterranean flora. However, 35 plants from the Mediterranean were grown at Munstead for inclusion in the plant nursery catalogue and a further eight from areas with a Mediterranean-type climate. She wrote at least 95 articles describing individual plants from this area, and her books contain many references to the plants of the Mediterranean. It is clear from these references that at Munstead and Munstead Wood she was growing and experimenting with many more plants from the Mediterranean than she made available commercially from the plant nursery.

A Mediterranean climate and the plants associated with it are found not only along the coasts of North Africa and southern Europe – the Mediterranean Basin proper – but also South Africa, parts of the Chilean and Californian coasts and South Australia. In terms of hardiness zones they lie between +4 and

– 12° C average minimum temperature, and plants adapted to these conditions can be found over a wider area in New Zealand, Tasmania and elsewhere. The typical climate of the Mediterranean is characterised by long hot, dry summers with average temperatures of 20-24° C and cool, wet winters of 4-7°C. In the countries around the Mediterranean Basin that Miss Jekyll visited, lower temperatures and wetter conditions occur in the mountains, and plants are adapted to the drying cold spring winds from the north – the Mistral in southern France, the Bora in the Adriatic and the Meltemi in the Aegean – or hot, dry winds from the south – the Sirocco in Africa. Similar strong but diurnal winds blow onshore and offshore along parts of the Californian coast. In addition the plants are adapted to a range of local conditions, such as exposure, proximity to the sea, rock type and soils, all of which Miss Jekyll noted.

On the face of it, successfully transferring plants from the Mediterranean to be grown outside in southern Britain would appear remote or serendipitous, but Miss Jekyll either succeeded where others had failed or made recourse to the use of the cool greenhouse. Theresa Earle noted in 1897 that, 'Miss Jekyll of Munstead Wood now sells her surplus plants, all more or less suited to light sandy soils, to the management of which she has for many years given special attention.' Herein lies the secret of Miss Jekyll's success for sandy soils which, though poor in nutrients, are quick draining and warm, and which can be enriched with humus for more demanding plants. Thus, once the iron pan which held up water in the Lower Greensand had been broken, the light sandy soils of this part of Surrey, east and west of Munstead, became well drained and warm. The construction of dry stone walls, garden walls, rockeries and clearings within woodland provided habitats comparable to those she had encountered in the Mediterranean countries she had visited between 1863 and 1883.

Her first excursion in 1863 when she was 19 years old (though she celebrated her 20th birthday in Constantinople) was in the company of Mary Newton and her husband Charles (later Sir Charles) Newton who was then Keeper of Greek and Roman Antiquities at the British Museum. The tour lasted for over two months and included visits to Rhodes, Turkey and Greece. As well as the buildings, classical ruins and people, she drew and noted the plants and vegetation. On Corfu, she remarked upon, '*the forest of magnificent wild olives with myrtles and everywhere cyclamens.*' A little later, on Rhodes, she records that she was '*very happy with the wild flowers – cyclamen, narcissus, crocus, iris and, whenever the rocks overhung and made cool places, the beautiful bright green Maidenhair Fern.*' This was the plant, *Adiantum capillusveneris*, that she was to grow thirty years later as a 'fringe' to the tank at Munstead Wood, and in 1927 she sent a frond of it as a Christmas greeting to the actress Amy Barnes-Brand at Woodhouse Copse whose garden she was designing.

Later, she wrote:

'*Mary and I had a walk in the afternoon on the north shore. The cyclamens that grow in the crevices of the rocks are delightful, and on the north side of every cool shady rock there is sure to be a fringe of the bright green maidenhair fern. There is a kind of prickly wild thyme [possibly Thymus capitatus] very aromatic. A number of the small wild plants and bushes are sweet and prickly, and in walking over the rough ground and crushing the plants underfoot there is always a sweet smell like thyme and myrtle.*'

Irids were already of great interest to her, and a visit to a Turkish cemetery on Rhodes displayed, as it does today, many irises amongst the graves. From here she took a root and wrote, '*it will go home with me, and I shall hope to make it grow.*' Many years later she identified it as *Iris albicans*.

On their return home via Athens, the Newtons and Miss Jekyll visited:

'*a fine shady garden, made by the late Queen, with many orange trees, Acacia, the pretty Pepper trees, Aloes, Pines, Arundo, and a few palms with a beautiful view of the Acropolis. I took a seed pod from a plant with deeply cut leaves. I had never seen it before, but it looked like some kind of Solanum, and I hoped to grow it at home as a remembrance of beautiful Athens.*'

Gertrude Jekyll made two further visits to the Mediterranean, the first in 1868 with a fellow student Susan Muir-Mackenzie of Delvine, Perthshire and the second in 1873 with her younger brother Herbert. They lasted only a few weeks each, but her next visit was for several months and was the longest time she ever spent away from England.

She spent the winter of 1873-1874 in Algiers with her friend, the artist Barbara Bodichon (née Leigh-Smith), sailing from Marseilles on 1st November 1873 and arriving at the Bodichon's home on Mustapha Supérieur three days later. A local botanist, Professor Durando, helped her explore the coast and inland to collect and draw plants. Francis Jekyll notes that no written

Gertrude Jekyll's watercolour of bougainvillea. (By kind permission of the Jekyll Trust).

record has survived, but there is a sketchbook at the Godalming Museum and an album of watercolours at the Surrey History Centre in Woking. From the latter, some eight watercolours were reproduced in 1998 in *Country Life*. Francis Jekyll described them in 1934, but William Robinson had already done so in *The Garden* in 1880. Under the nom de plume 'Justicia' he described them thus:

'There is much of plant interest shown incidentally in the sketches. A picturesque lane with great trees of Lentisk [possibly Pistacia Lentiscus] is also garlanded with the elegant winter-flowering Clematis cirrhosa – a precious plant for all those living in mild districts in this country; another sketch shows an immense belt of Prickly Pear forming a wide protection and fence to a village. Two things only penetrate this great and fierce growth, the common porcupine and the delicate pale yellow Clematis which garlands with beauty the great branches of the pear, and hangs from them in wreaths affording a most novel effect. Against a house there is a large and picturesque mass of Bougainvillea [which was reproduced on the cover of Country Life in March 1998], a mound of glorious colour; even more remarkable is an enormous bush of Poinsettia sketched in the garden of an Englishman, Mr. Arkwright; still more interesting, however, because like the clematis, useful in our own land, are the two beautiful winter-flowering Irises dotted about the foreground of the sketches. Their delicate grey-blue flowers make the desert and the ruin charming. It is pleasant to know that these flowers….bloom in the open air in our gardens in winter and early spring.'

These irids are *Iris alata*.

In 1876, Miss Jekyll visited Venice with her mother to see her elder sister and husband, and in 1883 she was in Capri staying with Lady Grantley of Wonersh. Other visitors were Mr. F. W. Burbidge and Herr. Max Leichtlin in whose company she identified, collected and drew plants growing on the island. Many of these were sent to Kew, to William Robinson and to Munstead. She wrote enthusiastically to William Robinson about one of her plant hunting expeditions:

'I wish you could have such a holiday as I am enjoying – an island with magnificent natural features, a charming population, primitive and unspoilt, and air so bracing and invigorating that one feels like a giant! I am generally a bad walker, but I find myself on my feet all day and the walking is hard work, up and down rocky steps for the most part. As for the plants it is a kind of intoxication to get into a wilderness of olive and myrtle, orange and prickly pear, and the rough ground clothed with Smilax, Cyclamens and Rosemary, and the many aromatic plants that grow in the Mediterranean islands, only one has to go carefully for one comes suddenly to nasty places when one looks over and sees the sea a thousand feet below! I hope to bring home some useful plants; my little tool [a pick for plant collecting designed by Miss Jekyll] has covered itself in glory, you should have seen it today picking and chipping out of the crevices of a cliff of white marble some sturdy plants of Campanula fragilis – it abounds near the sea. I can get plenty of that beautiful Lithospermum rosmarinifolia – if you know anyone who would like half a dozen plants by post I would send on getting a postcard.'

A plant that grows in Capri, central Italy and elsewhere in the Mediterranean that Miss Jekyll used at The Manor House for wall plantings was indeed *Lithospermum (Lithodora) rosmarinifolia*.

Lithospermum rosmarinifolia at The Manor House. Miss Jekyll first collected cuttings from this plant in Capri in 1883.

In January 1884 she sent flowering specimens to William Robinson as F. W. Burbidge had done the week before, and wrote:

'I send you flowers of Lithospermum rosmarinifolia. They are extremely fugacious when picked…This Lithospermum grows mostly on the limestone cliffs overhanging the sea, but happily also in more accessible places, nearly always in company with Rosemary, which it strongly resembles when out of flower.' She described it in the nursery catalogue as, *'one of the very best plants for rock or warm bank. Growth prostrate, flowers a pure and brilliant blue.'*

Another plant from the Mediterranean and much used in the garden at The Manor House is rosemary. From Capri she collected:

'the form of the rosemary known as Rosmarinus officinalis procumbens. [It] grows in crevices of exposed rocks near the sea; the branches are quite prostrate, hugging the rock and following all its forms. I have secured some seedling plants and rooted natural layers, wishing to prove if it will retain its prostrate form in cultivation. I am inclined to doubt it, observing that where it grows in better soil and shelter it is an upright bush, though less free in growth than our garden kind.'

At The Manor House, the upright form is used against stone retaining walls and in borders and she has deployed it as she did at Munstead Wood:

Left: Rosemary in flower at The Manor House.

Right: Cistus laurifolius and Rosa arvensis in the Wild Garden at The Manor House.

'I plant rosemary all over the garden, so pleasant is it to know that at every few steps one may draw the kindly branches through one's hand, and have the enjoyment of their incomparable incense; and I grow it against walls so that the sun may draw out its inexhaustible sweetness to greet me as I pass; and early in March, before any other scented flower of evergreen is out, it gladdens me with the thick setting of pretty lavender-grey bloom crowding all along the leafy spikes.'

Cistuses were a great favourite of Miss Jekyll, and she writes at length about them in two of her books *Home and Garden* and *Wood and Garden,* and there are a further six short articles about them in the gardening journals. At Munstead Wood, she grew cistuses not only with azaleas but also in a clearing with heather plants – the native ling to which she added *Erica ciliata,* Cornish Heath and the white form of Irish Heath *Daboecia polifolia [D. cantabrica f. alba].* Another association was with dwarf rhododendrons and Pieris, and a final one at Munstead was with free-growing roses, such as *R. polyantha* and *R. Brunonis [R. brunonii].* It is this final association that Miss Jekyll employed so effectively in the Wild Garden in The Manor House.

Cistus laurifolius flower at The Manor House.

141

Iris unguicularis at The Manor House.

more than 21 cultivars were supplied for the borders of the Formal Garden and a great many species for the Wild Garden. For the walls and narrow borders in the Formal Garden over one hundred *Iris stylosa [I. unguicularis]* were supplied. About this Algerian Iris she wrote on many occasions extolling its merits as a fragrant winter-flowering plant. She had collected it whilst staying with Barbara Bodichon in Algiers in 1873-4 and wrote about it in *Wood and Garden* 27 years later:

> 'What a delight it was to see *[Iris stylosa]* for the first time in the hilly wastes, a mile or two inland from the town of Algiers. Another lovely blue Iris was there too, Iris alata or scorpiodes, growing under exactly the same conditions; but this is a plant unwilling to be acclimatised in England. What a paradise it was for flower-rambles, among the giant Fennels and the tiny orange Marigolds, and the immense bulbs of Scilla maritima standing almost out of the ground, and the many lovely Bee-orchises and the fairy-like Narcissus serotinus, and the groves of Prickly Pear wreathed and festooned with the graceful tufts of bell-shaped flower and polished leaves of Clematis cirrhosa!'

At about the same time, an English resident of Algiers, the Rev. Edwyn Arkwright, had discovered a single plant of a white flowered variety of *Iris unguicularis* which he introduced to England via Wares of Tottenham, now available from only four suppliers.

Miss Jekyll did not restrict herself in her gardens at Munstead and Munstead Wood in the use and trials of plants from the Mediterranean area alone, but chose more widely from those areas with a Mediterranean-type climate. From South America came the Chilean Crocus (*Techophilaea cyanocrocus*) in 1872, which she described as 'perhaps the brightest pure blue flower we have,' at Munstead. From South Africa came *Agapanthus campanulatus*, which she described in *Country Life* in 1924, *Agathaea coelestis (Felicia amelloides)*, *Plumbago capensis* and *Kniphofia caulescens*. By 1883, at Munstead Miss Jekyll had over an hundred flowers of *K. caulescens* out simultaneously, and in an article in *The Garden* the following quotation indicates the success she had with this genus:

Borders at Munstead Wood were set aside for Irids, of which the Iris and Lupin Garden, west of the workshop was much admired and photographed. She used both Iris species and cultivars, and wrote enthusiastically about them. Of *Iris tuberosa [Hermodactylus tuberosus]* from the Levant she wrote in 1885:

> 'Do you know this wonderful little Iris, made of green satin and black velvet. Was it not Ruskin who wrote of Velasquez that his black contains more colour than many another painters' whole palette – not perhaps in those words, but with that sense? I think this little Snake's-head Iris must have taught Velasquez.'

In the Munstead Wood nursery catalogue only five species are listed together with Iris hybrids of yellow, lavender and purple flowers. But for The Manor House no less than 150 plants of *'the glory of the garden is the Tritomas [Kniphofia] which flourish here with unwonted vigour. They give brightness and warmth everywhere about the place, but they are not dotted about indiscriminately or repeated everywhere, on the contrary they are collected into bold masses in a few good positions, where their brilliancy lights up the surroundings.'*

And so it is in the Wild Garden today at the Manor House. From California came *Carpenteria californica*, first described by W. Gumbleton of Belgrove, Queenstown in 1880, acquired by Miss Jekyll in 1881 from Mrs Davidson and which flowered outdoors at Munstead in 1885. And from southern Australia and New Zealand came *Olearia x hastii, O. stellulata, O. Gunnii [O. phlogopappa]*, and *Veronica traversii [Hebe brachysiphon]*.

Notwithstanding this rich palette of plants from areas of the world that experience a Mediterranean-type climate, it was the plants and environments of the coasts of the Mediterranean basin that Miss Jekyll had visited between 1863 and 1884 that left a lifelong impression on her and that she used at Munstead and Munstead Wood and in her garden commissions. The impressions were visual, odoriferous and spiritual, and she extolled them in one of the chapters in *Wood and Garden* entitled 'The Scents of the Garden':

'But of all the sweet scents of bush or flower, the ones that give me the greatest pleasure are those of the aromatic class, where they seem to have a wholesome resinous or balsamic base, with a delicate perfume added. When I pick and crush in my hand a twig of bay, or brush against a bush of rosemary, or tread upon a tuft of thyme, or pass through incense-laden brakes of Cistus, I feel that here is all the best and purest and most refined, and nearest to poetry, in the range of faculty of the sense of smell.
The scents of all these sweet shrubs, many of them at home in dry rocky places in far-away lower latitudes, recall in a way far more distinct than can be done by a mere mental effort of recollection rambles of years ago in many a lovely southern land — in the islands of the Greek Archipelago, beautiful in form, and from a distance looking bare and arid and yet with a scattered growth of lowly sweet-smelling bush and herb, so that as you move among

them every plant seems full sweet sap or aromatic gum, and as you tread the perfumed carpet the whole air is scented; then of dusky groves of tall Cypress and Myrtle, forming mysterious shadowy woodland temples that unceasingly offer up an incense of their own surpassing fragrance, and of cooler hollows in the same lands and in the nearer Orient, where the Oleander grows like the willow of the north, and where the Sweet Bay throws up great tree-like suckers of surprising strength and vigour. It is only when one has seen it grow like this that one can appreciate the full force of the old bible simile. Then to find one standing (while still on earth) in a grove of giant Myrtles fifteen feet high, is like having a little chink of the door of heaven opened, as if to show a momentary glimpse of what good things may be beyond!'

Miss Jekyll included so many 'good things' of Mediterranean origin to see at The Manor House in Upton Grey, that we do indeed glimpse in their colours, textures, arrangements and fragrance, the good things that are beyond.

Kniphofia uvaria detail in the Wild Garden at The Manor House.

CHAPTER SEVEN

The Wild Garden

'One of the things most worthy of doing about a garden is to try to make every part of it beautiful; not the pleasure garden only, but some of the rougher accessories also, so that no place is unsightly.'

Opposite: Aerial view of The Manor House and surrounding countryside 1985. The just-under-five acre garden stands on sloping land with a pH of 7-8.

The Wild Garden, which covers about half of the just-under-five acre garden, is on the north-west side of the house. The architects' plan, dated September 23rd 1908, is included with those in the Reef Point Collection. It shows planting, most of which had been carried out between 1902, when Charles Holme bought The Manor House, and 1908, which is the date of the architects' plans.

In front of the house, what was to become Miss Jekyll's Wild Garden starts with an entrance where curved grass steps lead to a field in which are marked walnut trees, horse chestnuts, laburnum, weeping ash, laurel and a hedging of holly. The naturally spring-fed pond is at the far end, near the entrance to the garden from the road. From here the drive curves back gently between stands of horse chestnuts towards the house and stables. Levels are marked in red ink, but are not visible on our black and white copy.

The fact that the architects' plan is dated September 23rd 1908 shows that Miss Jekyll must have done a great deal of work in the last few months of that year because most of her plans are dated 1908; very few are 1909. We assume she referred to the architect's plans for gradients etc. when drawing her own. She drew only two plans for the Wild Garden, one is for the whole area and the other shows detailed pond planting.

There is however an alternative plan which applies to the entrance of the Wild Garden from the house. This shows two *Magnolia stellata* that stand on either side of the path which leads from the grass steps. Beyond these are two *Magnolia* x *soulangiana* 'Lennei.' In his *The International Book of Trees* Hugh Johnson describes this magnolia as *'perhaps the most splendid form of the most popular garden hybrid magnolia.'* It has huge flowers and was discovered in a garden in northern Italy

in 1850. I wonder if Miss Jekyll saw it growing in Italy on her travels in that area.

On this plan, which she labels 'Upton Grey Magnolia 1909', she also adds alternative planting of magnolia at the ends of Border 3 and Border 4 in the Formal Garden. As the date of these plans is one year later than the ones I have worked from, I hope I have elected to use her preferred design. Perhaps Charles Holme or Mr Best requested that she use magnolia (many are from Japan) but that would have been at the expense of losing some of the rambler roses that festoon the top of the Wild Garden's grass steps. In the Formal Garden I suspect the roots of the quite vigorous *Magnolia soulangia* that she planned in that area would have wreaked havoc in the dry-stone walls directly beneath.

We do not know whether Miss Jekyll worked entirely from the architects' plans or whether she visited the garden, but because no letters survive with the plans it is possible that she may have come here.

When we bought The Manor House in 1984, the Wild Garden was completely overrun with, brambles, other weeds, shrubs and small trees. Nearly all the photographs I took in the first few months mean nothing to me now as I cannot work out where they are taken from or look towards. Most of the horse chestnut trees along the drive had survived as had two walnut trees, one of which was blown over in the 1987 storm and the other, a seedling, was in the wrong place alongside the church wall. Clearing all and starting again on clean earth was far easier than planting amongst the survivors. Even the pond had disappeared under thick weeds, and its once waterproof clay base had cracked and no longer held water. Water table levels in this part of Hampshire have dropped dramatically over the past hundred years and there is now no sign of the spring that once fed the pond.

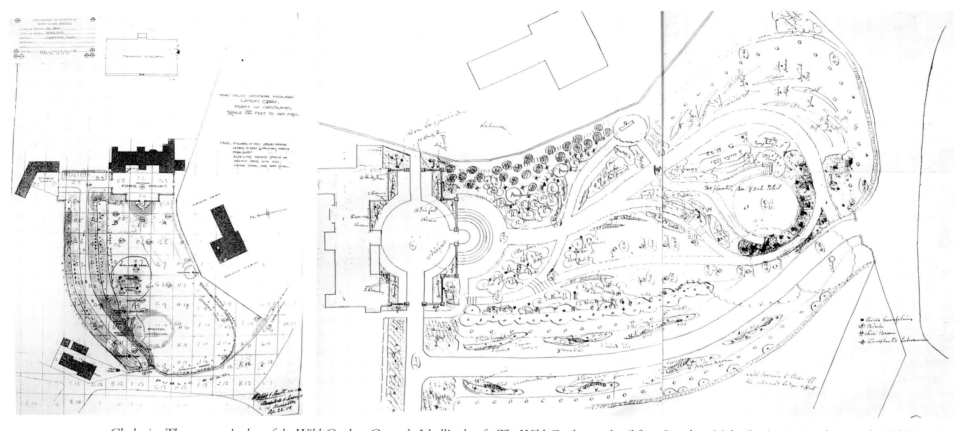

Clockwise: The surveyor's plan of the Wild Garden; Gertrude Jekyll's plan for The Wild Garden; a detail from Jonathan Myles-Lea's painting showing the Wild Garden; Gertrude Jekyll's plan for planting along the drive; Gertrude Jekyll's alternative plan for the entrance to the Wild Garden and for the two ends of Borders 3 and 4.

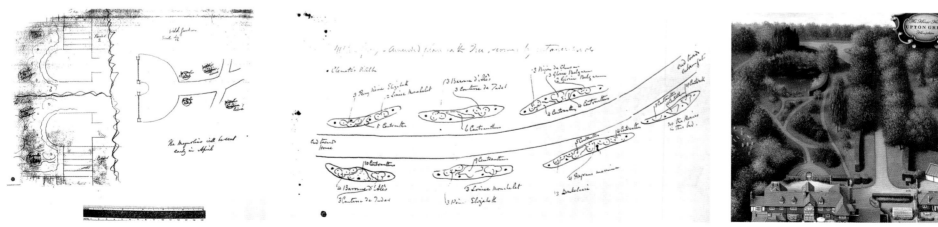

146

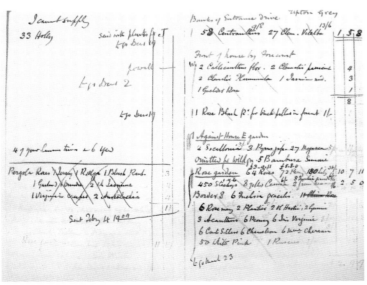

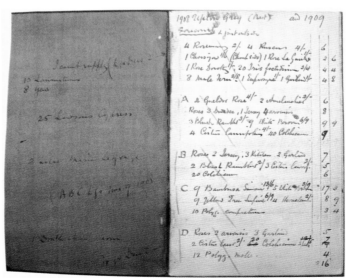

Above left: From the far end of the Wild Garden towards the house in 1984.

Above right: The entrance to the Wild Garden in 1984.

Below left: Munstead Wood nursery's plant list for the Wild Garden forecourt.

Below right: Munstead Wood nursery list for plants at the entrance to the Wild Garden.

THE DRIVE

The drive from the road to the house runs along one side of the Wild Garden and is lined with horse chestnut trees [*Aesculus hippocastanum*]. Miss Jekyll's plans show an under-planting of tree peonies at the feet of the chestnut trees along both sides of the drive. Today it would simply not be possible to grow any herbaceous plants at the feet of the now very large, shading, trees. Even the grass struggles to survive, so we have not attempted to restore those seven beds and I have the approval of fine gardeners for that omission.

Right: The drive and Aesculus hippocastanum *[Horse chestnut] under snow.*

Opposite: The drive from the entrance.

148

THE WILD GARDEN TODAY

'Wild gardening is delightful….but no kind of gardening is so difficult to do well.' Wood and Garden

The entrance to the Wild Garden from the house is through beautiful wrought-iron Arts and Crafts gates which are set beneath a semi-circular frame which is very frail and probably early seventeenth century. Beyond these, three shallow, curved grass steps lead to a grass path that meanders towards the pond. This branches out twice into narrower paths that run through long grasses and wild flowers into the surrounding garden making a walk through the Wild Garden longer and more interesting, so that the stroller can see every part from nearly every angle.

Our first job in this part of the garden was to grid the area into 10 feet squares and mark them with poles. This helped verify that plants and the restored pond were re-established in exactly the right places.

Today the Wild Garden has almost matured. Of course it takes

Right: The Wild Garden in spring. Grass paths wind gently into the distance between daffodils and wild flowers. The effect is attractive for a short season, but Miss Jekyll had the good sense to plant her daffodils in drifts at the far end of the Wild Garden so that the eye was drawn in that direction. Today they have multiplied and probably been added to by later generations and the effect is rather gaudy.

Opposite: The entrance to the Wild Garden in July. The shallow grass steps make a perfect entrance from the wrought iron gates.

Opposite: Overlooking the Wild Garden in June. Although the Wild Garden covers only about one-and-a-half acres, the winding paths make the walk through longer and more interesting. The planting becomes more free and natural as it leads towards the distant pond and on into nature.

Above left: The Wild Garden in June.

Below left: The same view in autumn.

Below right: The Wild Garden in mid-winter. These photographs show how nature in the Wild Garden changes with the seasons and always retains some beauty.

Right: The shallow steps that enter the Wild Garden.

Opposite:
Above right: Rosa 'Blush Rambler' 1903.
Above far right: Rosa 'The Garland' 1835.
Below left: Rosa 'Dundee Rambler' 1850.
Below middle: Rosa 'Jersey Beauty' 1899.
Below right: Rosa 'Euphrosyne' 1895.

years for three-foot trees and small shrubs to grow to their full size, and for the first few years of our opening the garden several visitors expressed dismay, saying that the rather young, controlled Wild Garden was no more wild than their own gardens. Now the maturing trees, shrubs, wild flowers and pond demonstrate the natural beauty of a Gertrude Jekyll Wild Garden.

William Robinson claimed that this gardening 'occasions no trouble.' As Penelope Hobhouse wisely warned me, it takes a great deal of care and vigilance to keep a wild garden disciplined, free and beautiful. Plants that are strong enough to be considered wild may also be dangerously vigorous, as I soon discovered.

Right: The Wild Garden entrance in late May with lilac beyond the wall and Olearia gunnii [O. phlogopappa] this side.

Below: Lilac 'Mme Lemoine' flower.

On entering the Wild Garden you walk through rambling roses that surround the curve at the top of the steps. In June and July they present a spectacular and colourful welcome to the visitor. The four roses are Rosa 'Blush Rambler', Rosa 'Dundee Rambler', Rosa 'The Garland' and Rosa 'Jersey Beauty', all of which are also planted on the pergola in the Formal Garden on the other side of the house.

Miss Jekyll wrote admiringly of rambler roses and she used them repeatedly in the larger gardens that she was asked to design. Their habit of holding long flexible canes headed with clusters of small flowers makes them ideal for covering arbours, pergolas and arches. Miss Jekyll described these roses as free-growing and wrote about one of her favourites, 'The Garland', in *Roses for English Gardens*:

'Of the old cluster roses, the one I have found the prettiest and most generally useful is The Garland, for it is beautiful in all ways.'

She advises their use on arches, for covering an arbour, or, as she describes, *'best of all as a natural fountain.'* And that fountain effect is evident in this wild garden because, like all ramblers, it throws up flowering shoots from the base to give the effect of a fountain, first rising then tumbling down around itself.

These old ramblers flower only once each summer, but that flowering is so amazingly profuse that, grouped together as they are, they prove their worth in those few glorious weeks. She explained this close planting:

'I think it desirable to group together flowers that bloom at the same time. It is impossible, and even undesirable, to have a garden in blossom all over, and groups of flower-beauty are all the more enjoyable for being more or less isolated by stretches of intervening greenery.'

Two other roses grow beyond these. One is Rosa 'Euphrosyne', a very pretty pale pink rambler which I bought from André Êve in France as it was not available in England, and the other, a rose which is now lost called 'Kitchener'. I am told that although Miss Jekyll did use that rose in some of her gardens it never passed the tests that are required for a plant to reach commercial production. That is another example of Miss Jekyll's adventurous use of new plant material. She realised that gardeners who were not prepared to expand their art were limited because they ignored *'the immense resources that are the precious possession of modern gardeners.'* That precious possession included the plants that were arriving in Britain with plant-hunters from around the world.

Three lilacs grow behind the roses on one side of the grass path. As Miss Jekyll simply wrote 'Lilac' on the plan I have planted one white Syringa 'Madame Lemoine', a fine old

Left: In the middle of the Wild Garden with species roses, Rosa virginiana and Rosa arvensis.

Above right: Rosa virginiana bush.

Below right: Rosa virginiana flower.

157

Right: Walnuts on Juglans regia.

Opposite: In the centre of the Wild Garden towards the Juglans regia [Walnuts].

variety, and two other lilacs, *Syringa vulgaris*. The latter need controlling as they sucker from roots with abandon.

On each side of the drive a holly hedge [*Ilex aquifolium*] grows and horse chestnut trees [*Aesculus hippocastanum*] line the drive within the hedges. Seven ilex have been added to the hedge, beside which Miss Jekyll notes '*Add hollies to take off the straight edge effect.*'

The precept of a wild garden was that it should start with a little formal structure and then blend into nature at the end of the garden. At Upton Grey Miss Jekyll followed the rambling roses with species roses, *Rosa arvensis* and *Rosa virginiana* (which she knew as *Rosa lucida*). The latter does tend to spread but in winter months the bright red stems and hips make up for its wandering habit and it is quite easily controlled.

A group of walnut trees [*Juglans regia*] grows in the centre of the Wild Garden. When they are fully mature they will form a very small copse. To me that represents our piece of the woodland which Miss Jekyll so loved. A planting of bamboo Simonii [*Pleioblastus simonii*], tree lupins and white broom [*Cytisus*] grow opposite within a loop in the path that leads to a weeping ash [*Fraxinus excelsior pendula*]. I chose to use *Cytisus* x *kewensis* for its very pale, almost white, flowers. It is not happy on our thin chalky soil and I have to replace dead plants every two or three years.

Beyond this there are two further plantings of bamboo; these are marked as Bamboo Metake [*Pseudosasa japonica metake*]. Both Pseudosasa and Pleioblastus are the running types of bamboo, and their roots can spread a metre or more a year. Those plants, together with *Polygonum japonicum* var *compactum* and *Polygonum molle* and Giant Hogweed [*Heracleum mantegazzianum*] make the area, as Penelope Hobhouse forewarned me in 1984, hard to control.

Left: Bamboo simonii [Arundinaria simonii] in the centre of the Wild Garden. Bamboo were a popular introduction to gardens of Miss Jekyll's era. Today newer, less invasive varieties are used. The two that Miss Jekyll chose for this garden were among the very few plants that had survived the century when we arrived in 1984. I treasured them for a very short time but was all too soon aware of their disturbingly invasive habit. I keep them under strict control but will not change them because this is a faithful restoration.

Right: Detail of the bamboo with foxgloves.

Below left: Laburnum anagyroides along the church wall in the Wild Garden.

Below right: Bamboo simonii under snow.

Opposite: Weeping Ash [Fraxinus excelsior] with Rosa 'Jersey Beauty'.

Above left: Rosa Mme d'Arblay.

Above right: Snowdrop [Galanthus nivalis]. One of the many varieties of galanthus that we found in the wild garden – where they flourish and multiply annually.

Opposite: View from the Wild Garden back to the house through wild flowers and grasses in June.

Along the church wall *Prunus lusitanica* and laburnum [*Laburnum anagyroides*] grow. On her plans Miss Jekyll has written '*transplanted laburnum*'. That usually means her client brought some of his plants with him when he moved house, or that he was already growing those in situ, or elsewhere on his property. If her client was Charles Holme, I wonder if Red House was denuded of laburnum when he moved to Upton Grey.

When the yellow panicles of the laburnum are in flower simultaneously with the yellow tree lupins below, the effect is quite dramatic; one rich yellow candelabra hanging down, the other spiralling up.

I have allowed a pretty rambler rose, Rosa 'Madame d'Arblay' (1835), to stay growing where I found it in 1984. It does not interfere with Miss Jekyll's plants or disfigure her plan.

Cistus laurifolius is planted in small groups in this area. It is evergreen and is from the Mediterranean area but is hardy in Hampshire. On hot days the leaves and stems give off a pleasant, incense-like scent.

Three silver birch [*Betula pendula*] are planted inside the drive's western holly hedge beside one branch of the grass path. A sorbus, which Miss Jekyll called Whitebeam, and a flowering cherry [*Prunus plena*] are planted near the birch.

THE POND AREA

'Make no parade of conscious effort.' Wood and Garden

Noting the importance of autumn colour in the Wild Garden Gertrude Jekyll advised the use of *'variety of growth and changeful schemes of colour'* in her book *Gardens for Small Country Houses.*

At the second cross-junction of the main path the plans show what looked to me like four *Polygonum compactum [Fallopia japonica* var *compacta]*. This is a variety of the horrendously invasive Japanese Knotweed. It is also planted beside the pond where I believe I have more chance of controlling it; so I have planted the Knotweed there and, instead of the four at the junctions in the centre of the Wild Garden I have put two

Opposite: Across the pond towards the church in early summer.

Right: Across the pond toward the house in early June. Iris orientalis line one edge and at the far side to the right Aruncus dioicus (known to Miss Jekyll as A. sylvester) is just appearing.

Above: Across the pond towards the church in August. Now the aruncus is in flower. We keep the seed-heads through the winter as they still have a feathery beauty.

Right: Gertrude Jekyll's plan for the pond area.

Far right: Polygonum campanulatum. This is a form of Japanese knotweed but is not as extremely invasive as Polygonum cuspidatum.

Opposite: Aruncus sylvester [A. dioicus] at the pond.

Aruncus dioicus sylvester which is a large, beautiful and well-behaved plant. (Miss Jekyll planted this, at the side of the pond). In the other two spaces I have planted the pretty and controllable *Polygonum molle*.

As the Knotweed had quite recently been introduced to Britain when Miss Jekyll was designing gardens it is assumed that she was not immediately aware of the danger of using it. But she soon realised that it would become troublesome.
She wrote:

'It is a good thing that we have a Polygonum [P. campanulatum] of moderate height which is not only a beautiful border plant, but is not a deep-rooting and over-growing invader such as all gardeners have suffered from the case of P. cuspidatum and its still worse variety, Polygonum cuspidatum compactum, a plant that when once established becomes an ineradicable pest.'

I was given what I believed was the planned polygonum in 1985 (by a friend who also did not know its potential danger, but who, like Miss Jekyll admired its form). Recently Professor Michael Tooley told me to look closer at our plans for the Wild Garden. He believes the word that follows Polygonum is 'campanulatum' not 'compactum'. On inspection I think he may well be correct. Miss Jekyll's writing is tricky to decipher and I trust Michael. He has always been right in the past. I shall take care to control our polygonum by putting a strong herbicide down the hollow stems where it runs out of its

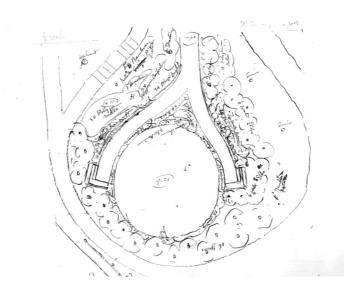

Above left: Helleborus niger. Hellebores are such good plants. Their range of species could provide a good display throughout the year. If I could have only one genus it would probably be this.
Above right: Helleborus orientalis.
Below left: Polygonum molle [Persicaria mollis]. I can forgive this one's gently wandering habit. It is very pretty when in flower.
Below right: Iris orientalis.
Opposite: Polygonum molle at the pond.

planned area. It has been sitting by the pond for nearly thirty years now, so is waiting a long time if it intends to invade us. I expect I was given the less invasive campanulatum.

Other plants that surround the pond include more *Bamboo simonii* [*Pleioblastus simonii*], and bamboo metake [*Arundinaria metake*] [*Pseudosasa japonica* metake], *Iris foetidissima*, Lent hellebores [*Helleborus niger* and *H. orientalis*] day lilies [*Hemerocallis fulva*], tansy [*Tanecetum vulgare*], meadowsweet [*Filipendula ulmaria*], monarda, *Iris orientalis* and *Iris pseudacorus*, geranium, *Polygonum molle* [*Persicaria mollis*], kniphofia, and crocus [*Colchicum*]. *Polygonum molle*, although also invasive, is not uncontrollable and is very pretty in late summer when frizzles of small white flowers cover it.

Two of Miss Jekyll's favourite crab-apple trees, Malus 'Dartmouth' and Malus 'John Downie', three standard quince *[Cydonia vulgaris]*, a medlar *[Mespilus germanica]* and several water elder *[Viburnum opulus]* grow near the pond.

Top left: Quince [Cydonia oblonga].
Top right: Medlar [Mespilus germanica].
Left: Water Elder [Viburnum opulus] berries. All these trees were used time and again by Miss Jekyll, and have a lovely old-fashioned comfort about them, although the two edible fruits, quince and medlar are rarely used today.
Opposite: Water Elder [Viburnum opulus] at the pond's edge with Polygonum campanulatum in the foreground.

Above: Giant Hogweed [Heracleum mantegazzianum] flower head.

Right: Giant Hogweed plant (eight feet tall!). This makes a beautiful and natural feature in the Wild Garden from June until the end of summer. It is important to remove the seed-head before it sets seed because it is considered a noxious weed.

Gertrude Jekyll also planned Giant Hogweed [*Heracleum mantegazzianum*], another very invasive plant, to grow near the pond. But heracleum is controllable if I cut off its magnificent head before it goes to seed and, until it does, it makes a fine tall focal point in the Wild Garden.

A small hedging of yew grows on the north side of the pond.

In the grass beyond the pond Miss Jekyll has planted drifts of daffodils, some of which I have not been able to trace. Daffodils are a narcissus. I am told that word is taken from the Greek 'narke' meaning numbness, torpor, for its narcotic properties. Daffodil bulbs are certainly quite poisonous to some creatures, which probably accounts for their survival over the centuries and also for the survival of hundreds of other narcissi that seem to have been added to the Wild Garden by subsequent residents. Those I have not been able to find are N. 'Leedsi' (possibly N. 'amabilis'), N. 'Barri conspicuous' and N. 'Nora Barton'. I think we have the following, all of which are division 1, trumpet; N. 'Emperor', N. 'Empress' and N. 'Horsfieldii'. All are planted in drifts that run towards to churchyard wall, just beyond which Charles Holme is buried. I believe that Miss Jekyll might have felt, as I feel, that a garish display of bright yellow daffodils running all over the Wild Garden is unnecessary. Her few, small drifts are planted at the very far end of the Wild Garden. The entrance and centre of the Wild Garden was left to waving green, pale-purple grasses and delicate wild flowers.

The garden ends at the village road with a screening of Chestnut trees, Irish yew [*Taxus baccata 'Fastigiata'*] and *'laurels replanted loosely.'* Miss Jekyll, leaving the things she considered important in place, did not disturb the two-thousand-year old yew tree at the entrance to the drive.

Group of daffodils in the Wild Garden where, because their bulbs are poisonous to most creatures, they thrive and multiply.

CHAPTER EIGHT

The Art Completed

'The love of gardening is a seed that once sown, never dies but grows to an enduring and ever-increasing source of happiness.' Wood and Garden

If written by a twenty-first century gardener these words could sound like hyperbole, but they were written by stern, un-emotional Miss Jekyll in her first book *Wood and Garden*, published when she was aged 56 in 1899.

In the 28 years that I have been restoring and opening the garden she designed in 1908-09 it is that spirit of happiness that I have felt and shared with thousands of other gardeners from around the world. I have certainly learnt that gardening can be a frustrating, sometimes wilfully belligerent, but fulfilling pastime, and even in tough times it can be remarkably healing.

There is rarely a day when I wake without a project to start or complete. The reward is the breathtaking beauty, and sometimes the unexpected glory, of nature in the managed garden. It may have the same effect on the spirit that a piece of music has. It makes an impact on the mood of the recipient.

I have described Miss Jekyll's art as I understand it and have written about the reason for, and method of, restoring it as accurately as possible. I hope that, with this visual record, the garden can remain a testament to Gertrude Jekyll's knowledge, understanding of nature, and to her art.

The spirit of a fine artist often lives through the art and Miss Jekyll's spirit has imprinted itself on me as I work with her plans. The more I read her books the more I understand her love of nature, and in her garden at Munstead Wood, despite her terrible eyesight, how acutely she observes, and how well she describes, nature. In *Wood and Garden* she writes of her woodland's endless beauty even in the harsh

Two Pekin bantams.

month of February:

'There is always in February some one day, at least, when one smells the yet distant, but surely coming summer. Perhaps it is a warm, mossy scent …or a woodland opening, where the sun has coaxed out the pungent smell of trailing ground ivy.'
'How strangely little of positive green colour is to be seen in copse and woodland. Only the moss is really green. The next greenest thing is the northern sides of the trunks of beech and oak. Walking southward all are green, but looking back they are silver-grey.' *'In summer one never really knows how beautiful are the forms of the deciduous trees. It is only in winter, when they are bare of leaves, that one can fully enjoy their splendid structure and design.'*

She noticed those changing colours and shapes as the Impressionists understood them and her writings were, at times, so lyrical that they were like literary versions of Impressionist paintings. Vincent van Gogh's letters to his brother Theo sometimes describe the colours he sees in nature. They seem quite surprising at times, until you look as if through his eyes at the same feature.

She had a formidable intellect combined with exceptional artistic talent and determined self-assurance. She was able to communicate with people on many levels, from the children for whom she wrote *Children and Gardens* to the young factory lad who wrote to her asking advice on the planting of his window box. She took his letter seriously, replying

The bantams in the kitchen garden pergola in snow. Bantams are a constant source of amusement, pleasure and often grief. Being small they do little damage to a large garden so they run free in daylight. At night they are penned in for safety. They are relatively intelligent birds and can become friendly individual characters. But they do not pay their way in eggs as they lay only during the summer months and they are vulnerable to rats, foxes and some birds of prey. Gertrude Jekyll kept chickens, which, we are told, were allowed to range free during the years of World War I.

Over the Formal Garden in mid-winter when the importance of design becomes apparent.

both with advice and with material for his miniature garden. In *Children and Gardens* she advised her young readers:

'If you take any flower you please and look it over and turn it about and smell it and feel it and try to find out all its little secrets, not of flower only but of leaf, bud and stem as well, you will discover many wonderful things. This is how to make friends with plants and very good friends you will find them to the end of our lives.'

Edwin Lutyens wrote of her with affection and respect in his introduction to *Gertrude Jekyll, a Memoir*, the book written by her nephew Francis (and which, with his love of a pun, Lutyens later described as 'rather deadish'). It was published by Jonathan Cape in 1934, two years after her death in 1932. Lutyens described briefly the long friendship they shared:

'It was in 1889 that Mr Harry Mangles asked me to meet

his remarkable friend, Miss Jekyll. [Edwin Lutyens was then 20 and Miss Jekyll was 45]. *I eagerly accepted the privilege. She was already celebrated in the gardening world, and by her ever-growing circle of devoted and appreciative admirers.*

We met at a tea-table, the silver kettle and the conversation reflecting rhododendrons.

She was dressed in, what I learnt later to be, her Go-to-Meeting Frock – a bunch of cloaked propriety topped by a black felt hat, turned down in front and up behind, from which sprang alert black cock's-tail feathers, curling and ever prancing forwards [see page 8].

Quiet and demure, of few words and those deliberately chosen and deliberately uttered in a quiet, mellow voice – with keen, bright eyes that missed little in their persistent observation.

She spoke no word to me, but on leaving, with one foot on the step of her pony-cart and reins in hand, she invited me to

The orchard in spring. The pears blossom first and can be hit by a late frost.

Munstead on the very next Saturday. I was there on the tick of four, and was received by a somewhat different person – very much at home, genial and communicative, dressed in a short blue skirt that in no way hid her ankles, and the boots made famous through their portraiture by W. Nicholson; a blue linen apron with its ample marsupial pocket full of horticultural impedimenta; a blue-striped linen blouse box-pleated like a Norfolk jacket, the sleeves fastened close to her round wrists, giving her small and characteristic hands full freedom. She wore a straw hat turned up and down back and front, trimmed with a blue silk bow and ribbon.

I was shown all – the Garden and the Workshop – and was presented to her gracious Mother, with whom she then lived.

Such was the beginning of a friendship that lasted some forty-four years, during which my affection and admiration were ever-growing – only to end by the closing of that inevitable shutter called death.

Mrs Jekyll, of an older school, was courteous, gently considerate and patient with Gertrude's friends – gardeners, artists, architects, and all such as worked with hand and brain and came to her daughter for help, discussion and advice. It also led to a knowledge of that wise counsellor and gifted friend – her brother, Sir Herbert Jekyll.

My first visit led to many more, and the weekend at Munstead

The dogs and the bantams in the Kitchen Garden.

became a habit, and gave the opportunity for many a voyage of discovery throughout Surrey and Sussex, within a range possible to Bessie and the pony-cart she drew.

Old houses, farm-houses and cottages were searched for and their modest methods of construction discussed; their inmates and the industries that supported them. Many friends were found and unearthed and their lives and aims revealed.

Then followed the excitement of building her future home, Munstead Wood, wherein the business of building became a witty and exciting sport, with full discussions and great disputations. She was never ruffled save, perhaps, when asked a second question before the first was answered, and then her ruffle was more in the nature of sorrow than of anger.

Once I had the misfortune unconsciously to pick a flower marked for seed. Her gentle reprimand could but be likened to the story of Newton and his little dog. Such was the effect on me of her distress that I have never picked a flower since.

Her labours were multifarious and in them she was indefatigable and bore with great fortitude the persisting worry that her ever-shortening eyesight brought her.

She was musical and her keen hearing brought distress, and any sharp, quick noise lacking musical cadence gave her real pain, disturbing her usual equanimity and sweet temper.

Her wit and intelligent sympathy to all who worked with, for, and under her, adorned that world she made her own.

Her unfailing modesty and self-possession and her faith in that godliness from which she knew the best alone could spring, gave her the courage and the bearing that essentially pertains to one that can be described fitly as a grande dame.

A clear, logical brain, without favour or fear, save of God, for whose knowledge she for ever searched and which she now for ever shares.'

In an introduction to the same book Agnes Jekyll, the wife of Gertrude's favourite brother Herbert, acknowledged the difficulties for women of her time in a male dominated society.

'No one had a kinder heart, a more generous hand, a readier response for those who came asking help from her stores of

knowledge and experience, and the letters which poured in from all parts of the world when she died give abundant witness to this side of her character.

For Gertrude Jekyll was a pioneer spirit. Long before women had claimed their present independence in the arts and professions, in trade, in travel, in sport, and in many difficult crafts, she had quietly and firmly established her right to self-expression. Victorian heads, after years of deprecatory shaking, had at last to accept the inevitable. Men and women who had for the greater part made themselves famous in their varied walks of life, gave and called for her friendship, and her diaries and sketch-books, her press contributions, books and letters, all record ceaseless activities in many varied directions, bearing witness to exceptional powers of hand and brain united to any outlook in advance of her contemporaries. In her many books will be found, by those who are to seek them, the fruits of her practical experience, the sympathetic help of a fellow-worker, the contagious enjoyment of a writer of fine and simple English prose.'

Perhaps both Agnes and Gertrude were early feminists.

An obituary that appeared in *The Times* on December 12th 1932, credited Miss Jekyll with making an important contribution to garden art and horticulture. But it included William Robinson, who was to die three years later aged 97, a man, and although a very important figure in horticulture, no greater than Miss Jekyll.

'She was a great gardener, second only, if indeed she was second, to her friend William Robinson, of Gravetye. To these two, more than any others, are due, not only the complete transformation of English horticultural method and design, but also that wide diffusion of knowledge and taste which has made us almost a nation of gardeners. Miss Jekyll was also a true artist with an exquisite sense of colour.'

After a brief description of her early childhood the obituary added:-

'A succession of German and French governesses of the early Victorian type left no more than a resentful impression on her

independent mind and character. A brief incursion into boarding school life only deepened her sense of aloofness, and yet no one had a kinder heart, a more truly helpful and sympathetic spirit, a readier sense of humour and good comradeship.'

She was a strong and independent character. Her father called his child *'my oddity Gertrude'.*

We bought The Manor House in 1984. It took some time for the importance of the garden to dawn on me. The fact that no other Gertrude Jekyll garden, with the exception of the much smaller Lindisfarne, had been completely restored to her plans made the job of restoring this garden from dereliction to today's glory far less daunting to a beginner. It was a very exciting challenge. Energy and enthusiasm combined with enlightened encouragement from people who are expert in the subject are often the best fuels for success.

Restoring our Gertrude Jekyll garden to her 1908-09 plans has been an adventure into discovering very rare plants, meeting interesting fellow gardeners from around the world, and into a fascinating field of knowledge of both plants and their history.

One, perhaps the greatest, adventure has been in discovering plants that I believed lost, nurturing those treasures, and then planting them in their correct positions in the garden. Two of the most rare treasures that Upton Grey's garden holds are the hybrid tea rose, Rosa 'Killarney' and *Gladiolus brenchleyensis,* both of which were, to me, like finding a Penny Black stamp, and both of which were given to me by fine, generous gardeners.

I have also learnt that very few things in nature are perfect. To some extent the garden is like the human body. It gets diseases, allergies and, of course, death in parts. These must be dealt with where possible and accepted where cure is not possible.

In 1908 Miss Jekyll, at the age of 65, was arguably at the peak of her career. She was an established figure in the world of gardening, writing and in society. She had published eight books by the end of that year and had written a further three with other authors. William Robinson had used her photographs for some of his publications and, since 1881, she had regularly contributed a great many articles to various horticultural magazines. She

designed gardens for clients, some of whom lived a good distance from Surrey, and that at times when transport was slow and probably tiring. Some gardens she visited, on others she worked from architects' plans. She drew her plans before modern devices like copying machines had been invented and when landscape measuring equipment was limited. Luckily for the gardening world Miss Jekyll kept her plans at Munstead Wood and sent her clients copies. For that reason nearly all her plans survive. When the contents of Munstead Wood were sold, Beatrix Farrand, an important American landscape gardener bought a great many plans, letters and albums. These she gave to the University of California at Berkeley, where they remain today.

By the year of her death in 1932 Gertrude Jekyll had designed almost four hundred gardens. Three were in the United States, one was in Canada, eight were in mainland Europe and several were in Ireland. In 1918 she helped with plans for eight war cemeteries. Where visits to gardens would have required a long journey she often relied on architects' plans, and towards the end of her life she was reluctant to travel at all.

The plant nursery, which she ran commercially for 35 years from 1897 until 1932, provided a large range of plants for clients. Notes that Miss Jekyll wrote at the edges of our plans say such-and-such a plant will be sent in spring. Judging by the plant lists held by Godalming Museum she supplied a substantial quantity of plants for Upton Grey, and evidently she was also responsible for their delivery. Her energy was extraordinary and her standards always exacting.

Miss Jekyll's great nephew, Martin McLaren, wrote this astute comment in a letter to Lady Freyburg in 1948. 'If one had to put her gifts into one word it would have to be her genius for design.' He underlined design and I entirely agree. His widow, Nancy McLaren, has kindly allowed me to quote from his letter.

Miss Jekyll's restored Upton Grey garden is living evidence of her enduring art, and considering it as art of its era, it is remarkably innovative. She believed that art should progress and evolve with time and new plant discoveries. It is evidence of her open mindedness that she was able to use the newly discovered plants that were arriving in England from around the world and to incorporate such a large palette of material

into her gardens. She was well aware of the change that the seasons have on a garden and that, because it is composed of living material, it changes, both seasonally and with age.

She planned gardens accordingly, using plants and structure that can perform well in their turn throughout the seasons. Where inevitable death occurs Miss Jekyll used 'devices', as she called them, to fill the gaps. She would bend taller plants to spaces where a plant had died back, or plant a later flowering perennial near the spot of one that flowered earlier. Sometimes she introduced planted terracotta pots or a few correctly coloured annuals in order to continue failing drifts of early perennials. She appreciated the beauty and value of the large range of annuals available. Working with her plans I have also learnt to love those simple and rewarding annuals. She wrote on our plans *'filling snaps'* (antirrhinum) and advised gardeners to *'allow for death'*, in other words not to rely on the bedding out

The entrance to the Kitchen Garden through a rose arbour in June.

system which William Robinson described as *'leaving the beds thrice yearly like newly dug graves.'*

Upton Grey may be considered small in relation to many of her gardens but it is complete and it reveals a great many facets of the art of a mature and confident artist. Gertrude Jekyll understood plants and their needs. She was also a very practical gardener.

When giving talks about our garden I am often asked if I find following Miss Jekyll's plans inhibiting or restrictive. The answer is that I do not. Walking in the footsteps of a great artist is rewarding and I do not believe I can improve on her art. But Miss Jekyll's plants do have wills of their own. They certainly do not enjoy being supervised, in other words being allowed to flourish here but not to enter there. Nature does take some controlling and it is practised in the art of deception.

The fact that she photographed and wrote about her art in such detail makes it an art that can be seen and understood today. Very few gardens of earlier periods can be so faithfully restored, and of course, until the nineteenth century, no photographic recording of gardens and plants was possible.

I am also asked, by visitors from around the word, why Gertrude Jekyll is still so widely admired. I believe there are several reasons.

Opposite: Mark, Edith, dog and bantams. Hopefully Miss Jekyll's art will inspire future generations of gardeners.

Of importance is the fact that she was born at a time of great social change in Britain. The Industrial Revolution and the expansion of the British Empire bought wealth to the nation. This wealth was distributed widely among emerging middle class industrialists who needed to live near their places of work, in suitable houses surrounded by attractive gardens. The aristocracy, no longer the sole arbiters of taste, were encouraged to sell off parts of their large tenanted estates. This led to a boom in house building and a need for both architects and garden planners. Nineteenth-century plant hunters were collecting treasures from around the world. These were carefully transported with the help of new devices like the Wardian Case, then distributed among better-funded gardens, both private and botanic (particularly Kew, where research into growing and breeding new plants improved annually).

Knowledge of science in horticulture was advancing as was the introduction of garden machinery available for the smaller gardens.

New wealth lead to a better educated population who wished to read and learn about the art of gardening – an art that they could call their own; and increased prosperity led to more time for leisure pursuits.

Printing, including photographic printing, became cheaper and of a fine quality. This led to the publication of a large number of newspapers, magazines and books on every new popular subject, particularly gardening. All this important material, together with seeds and plants from the expanding number of plant nurseries, was efficiently transported throughout the British Isles by the newly laid railway network. The train probably made as important a contribution as any to the gardens of Britain.

Being a fashionable art made gardening both a hobby and a career that was attractive to women. With improved education women became aware that there was a fulfilling role for them outside marriage or spinsterhood. Women of Gertrude Jekyll's generation lived to see their sex contributing to society in a great many fields from medicine to politics.

To some extent horticulture, in its broadest context, is the most reliable recorder of mankind's evolution. Garden art from the earliest civilizations to today reflects changes in society, nature and climate. Evidence of disease, pestilence, war, poverty, education, health, wealth and power can be found in the combination of art and nature. Gardens and garden art thrive in good times, are neglected in hard times. So Miss Jekyll's 1908-09 garden at Upton Grey represents, not only garden art of its era, but the social conditions of certain classes and the extent to which plant hunters had ventured around the world in their quest to find and maintain treasures from foreign lands.

Few forms of art can satisfy all senses as completely as can art in the garden. A walk through a fine garden can stimulate strong emotions. In the garden nature provides the instruments, the gardener is the controlling conductor but the composer was the original artist. Miss Jekyll was the composer of Upton Grey's magnificent nature. Today, gardeners from around the world can view her art and judge its merit for themselves.

'It has taken me half a lifetime merely to find out what is best worth doing,
and a good slice out of another half to puzzle out the ways of doing it.'
— *Colour Schemes for the Flower Garden*

'But the lesson I have most thoroughly learnt and wish to pass on
is to know the enduring happiness that the love of gardening gives.'
— *Wood and Garden*

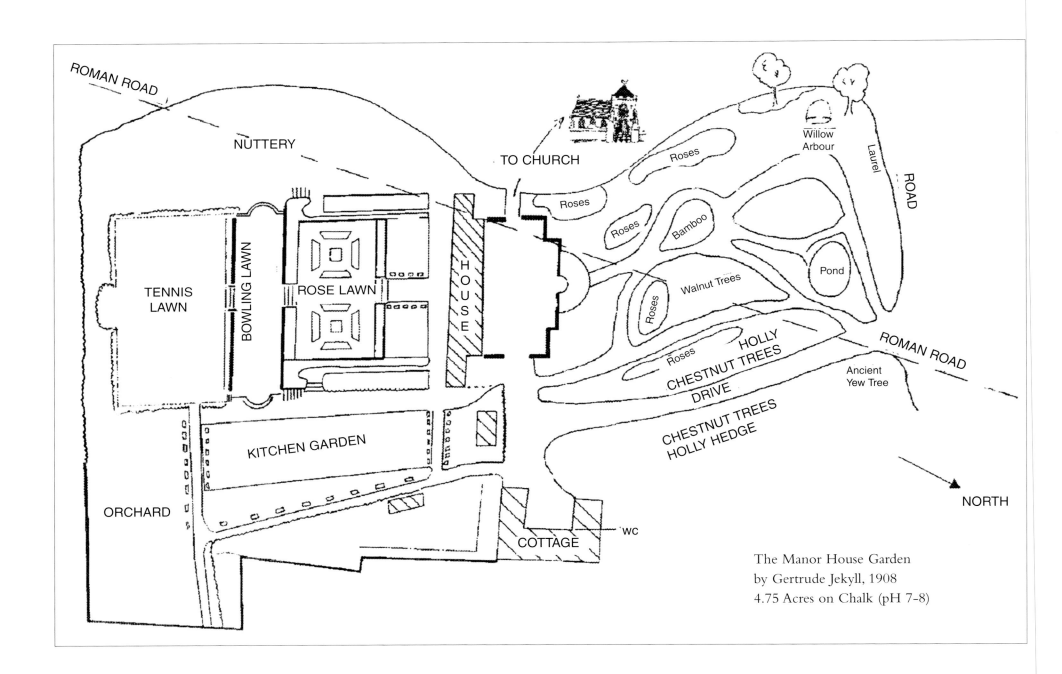

ROMAN ROAD

NUTTERY

TO CHURCH

Roses

Willow Arbour

Laurel

ROAD

Roses

Roses

Roses

Bamboo

BOWLING LAWN

TENNIS LAWN

ROSE LAWN

HOUSE

Pond

Roses

Walnut Trees

ROMAN ROAD

Roses

HOLLY

CHESTNUT TREES

Ancient Yew Tree

DRIVE

CHESTNUT TREES

HOLLY HEDGE

KITCHEN GARDEN

NORTH

ORCHARD

WC

COTTAGE

The Manor House Garden
by Gertrude Jekyll, 1908
4.75 Acres on Chalk (pH 7-8)

BIBLIOGRAPHY

Books

British and Japanese Biographical Portraits, The Japan Society, Routledge, Oxford, 2008

Jekyll, Francis, *Gertrude Jekyll: a Memoir,* Jonathan Cape Ltd., London, 1934

Jekyll, Gertrude, *Annuals and Biennials,* Country Life Ltd and G Newnes Ltd., London, 1916

Jekyll, Gertrude and Hussey, Christopher, *Garden Ornament,* Country Life Ltd and G Newnes Ltd., London, 1918

Jekyll, Gertrude and Mawley, Edward, *Roses for English Gardens,* Country Life Ltd and G Newnes Ltd., London, 1902

Jekyll, Gertrude, *Children and Gardens,* Country Life Ltd and G Newnes Ltd., London, 1908

Jekyll, Gertrude, *Colour in the Flower Garden,* Country Life Ltd and G Newnes Ltd., London, 1908

Jekyll, Gertrude, *Colour Schemes for the Flower Garden* (revised edition of above), Country Life Ltd., and G Newnes Ltd., London, 1914

Jekyll, Gertrude, *Home and Garden,* Longmans, Green & Co., London, 1900

Jekyll, Gertrude, *Wall and Water Gardens,* Country Life Ltd and G Newnes Ltd., London, 1901

Jekyll, Gertrude, *Wood and Garden,* Longmans, Green & Co., London, London, 1899

Johnson, Hugh, *The International Book of Trees*, Mitchell Beazley, London, 1973

King, Louisa Yeomans, *The Well Considered Garden,* Scribner, New York, 1915

Lasenby Liberty, Mrs Emma, *Japan: a Pictorial Record,* A & C Black, London, 1889

Leslie, George, *Our River*, Bradbury, Agnew & Co., London, 1888

Plant Finder, The, Royal Horticultural Society, London (annual publication)

Ruskin, John, *The Two Paths,* Smith, Elder & Co., London, 1859

Weathers, J, *A Practical Guide to Garden Plants,* Longmans, Green & Co., London, 1901

Magazines and Periodicals

Country Life Illustrated (founder Edward Hudson), London, 1897 –

Garden, The (founder William Robinson), London, 1871 -

Studio, The (founder Charles Holme), London, 1893-1964 (thereafter *Studio International*)

Times, The (founder John Walter), London, 1785 –

Traditional Home, Meredith Corporation, Iowa, USA, 1989 –

PLANT INDEX

Page numbers in *italic* refer to illustrations.

GENERAL INDEX

I wish to acknowledge and thank the following organisations who have
provided assistance and information in the research for this book:

The Surrey History Centre
www.surreycc.gov.uk/recreation-heritage-and-culture

The Gertrude Jekyll Estate
www.gertrudejekyll.co.uk

Guildford Museum, Surrey
www.guildford.gov.uk/museum

Godalming Museum, Surrey
www.waverley.gov.uk/godalmingmuseum

The Lutyens Trust
www.lutyens.org.uk